Dirty, Cheesy and Absolutely Awful Dad Jokes

Q: When do you kick a midget in the balls? A: When he is standing next to your girlfriend saying her hair smells nice

Q: What's the difference between your job and a dead prostitute? A: Your job still sucks!

Q: What did the hurricane say to the coconut palm tree? A: Hold on to your nuts, this is no ordinary blow job!

Q: How does a woman scare a gynecologist? A: By becoming a ventriloquist!

Q: What's 6 inches long, 2 inches wide and drives women wild? A: a $100 bill!

Q: What's long and hard and has cum in it? A: a cucumber

Q: How do you kill a circus clown? A: Go for the juggler!

Q: Did you hear about the guy who died of a Viagra overdose? A: They couldn't close his casket.

Q: Who was the world's first carpenter? A: Eve, because she made Adams banana stand

Q: Why does Dr. Pepper come (cum) in a bottle? A: Because his wife died!

Q: If a dove is the "bird of peace" then what's the bird of "true love"? A: The swallow.

Q: What do you call a cheap circumcision? A: a rip off Girl: "Hey, what's up?" Boy: "If I tell you, will you sit on it?"

Q: How do you get a nun pregnant? A: Dress her up as an altar boy.

Q: Why can't you play Uno with a Mexican? A: They steal all the green cards.

Q: Why don't orphans play baseball? A: They don't know where home is

Q: What's the difference between a Catholic priest and a zit? A: At least a zit waits until you're a teenager before it cums on your face!

Q: What does it mean when your boyfriend is in your bed gasping for breath and calling your name? A: You didn't hold the pillow down long enough.

Boy: "Want to hear a joke about my dick? Never mind, its too long." Girl: "Wanna hear a joke about my pussy? Never mind, you won't get it."

Q: How do you tell if a chick is too fat to fuck ? A: When you pull her pants down her ass is still in them

Q: What do you call 2 guys fighting over a slut? A: Tug-of-whore. Q: If the world is a Jacket where do poor people live? A: In the hood.

Q: What's the cure for marriage? A: Alcoholism.

Q: What do you call an anorexic bitch with a yeast infection? A: A Quarter Ponder with Cheese.

Q: Why do they call it PMS? A: Because Mad Cow Disease was already taken

Q: How do you stop a dog from humping your leg? A: Pick him up and suck on his cock!

Q: What's slimy cold long and smells like pork? A: Kermit the frogs finger

Q: What's a porn star's favorite drink? A: 7 Up in cider.

Q: What's the difference between a bowling ball and a blonde? A: You can only fit three fingers inside a bowling ball!

Q: What do priests and McDonalds have in common? A: They both stick there meat in 10 year old buns

Q: What do you call a white guy surrounded by 9 black guys? A: Steve Nash.

Q: Why can't Jesus play hockey? A: He keeps getting nailed to the boards.

Q: How do you circumcise a hillbilly? A: Kick his sister in the jaw.

Q: Why do men get their great ideas in bed? A: Because their plugged into a genius!

Q: What do you call an artist with a brown finger? A: Piccassole

Q: Did you guys hear about the cannibal that made a bunch of businessmen into Chili? A: I guess he liked seasoned professionals.

Q: What's the difference between a hooker and a drug dealer? A: A hooker can wash her crack and sell it again.

Q: Why was the guitar teacher arrested? A: For fingering A minor.

Q: Three words to ruin a man's ego...? A: "Is it in?"

Q: What's 72? A: 69 with three people watching

Q: What do the Mafia and a pussy have in common? A: One slip of the tongue, and you're in deep shit.

A redhead tells her blonde stepsister, "I slept with a Brazilian...." The blonde replies, "Oh my God! You slut! How many is a Brazilian?"

Q: Why don't black people go on cruises? A: They already fell for that trick once.

A daughter asked her mother how to spell penis, her mom said you should have asked me last night it was at the tip of my tongue.

Q: What has got two legs and bleeds? A: Half a dog!

Q: What do you call an afghan virgin A: Never bin laid on

Q: Why does Miss Piggy douche with honey? A: Because Kermit likes sweet and sour pork.

Q: What do you call a party with 100 midgets? A: A little get together.

Q: What is the difference between an illegal immigrant and E.T.? A: E.T. eventually went home!

Q: Why can't you hear a psychiatrist using the bathroom? A: Because the 'p' is silent

Q: Why did God give men penises? A: So they'd have at least one way to shut a woman up.

Q: What do you call a lesbian dinosaur A: A lickalotopis

Q: What's the difference between being hungry and horny? A: Where you put the cucumber.

What did the elephant say to a naked man? Hey that's cute but can you breathe through it?

Q: Did you hear about the celebrity murderer? A: He was shooting for the stars.

Q: What do girls and noodles have in common? A: They both wiggle when you eat them.

Q: What's the difference between roast beef and pea soup? A: Anyone can roast beef.

Q: Why did Tigger look in the toilet? A: Because he was looking for Pooh

If a firefighters business can go up in smoke, and a plumbers business can go down the drain, can a hooker get laid off?

Q: Do you know what the square root of 69 is? A: Ate something

If you had a donkey and I had a chicken and if your donkey ate my chicken what will you have? Three feet of my cock up your ass.

Q: What do you call a 13 year old girl from Kentucky who can run faster than her six brothers? A: A virgin.

Q: What kind of bees produce milk? A: Boobies

Q: Did you hear about the African American girl who was quiet during the movie? A: She wasn't

Q: What do you call two fat people talking? A: A heavy discussion.

Q: How do you start a parade in the ghetto? A: Roll a 40 down the street.

Q: What should you do if your girlfriend starts smoking? A: Slow down. And possibly use a lubricant.

Q: What's the worst thing about dating a blonde? A: If you don't know what hole to put it in neither do they.

Q: What did the penis say to the vagina? A: Don't make me cum in there.

Q: Why do women rub their eyes when they get up in the morning? A: They don't have balls to scratch.

Q: What do you call balls on your chin? A: A dick in your mouth!

Q: Did you hear about the Mexican racist? A: He joined the que que que.

Q: What do you call a man who cries while he masturbates? A: A tearjerker.

Q: What did the banana say to the vibrator? A: Why are YOU shaking? She's going to eat me!

Q: What's the difference between the Florida State football team and a Florida State cheerleader? A: They both suck for four quarters.

What's the difference between a rabbi and a priest? A rabbi cuts them off, A priest sucks them off

Q: Why do dwarfs laugh when they play soccer? A: The grass tickles their balls

Q: How do you rape a camel? A: One hump at a time.

Q: What do you call a bunch of retarded kids in a pool? A: Vegetable soup.

Q: What does a 75 year old woman have between her breasts that a 25 year old doesn't? A: Her navel.

Q: What does a good bar and a good woman have in common? A: Liquor in the front and poker in the back!

Q: What do you call a Spanish chick with no legs? A: Cuntswaylow

Q: Why did the semen cross the road? A: I wore the wrong socks today.

Q: Why does the Easter Bunny hide Easter eggs? A: He doesn't want anyone knowing he's been fucking the chickens!

Q: What's the difference between a hair stylist and a nail stylist? A: One does hand jobs and one does blow jobs!

Q: What is the difference between erotic and kinky? A: Erotic is using a feather....kinky is using the whole chicken.

Q: When does a cub become a boy scout? A: When he eats his first Brownie.

Q: What is the leading cause in death with lesbians? A: Hairballs.

Q: What did the cannibal do after he dumped his girlfriend? A: Wiped his ass.

Q: Did you hear about the butcher who backed into the meat grinder? A: He got behind in his work.

Q: What do you get when cross a donkey and an onion? A: a piece of ass that'll bring a tear to your eye!

Q: What does a woman and Kentucky Fried Chicken have in

common? A: By the time you're finished with the breast and thighs, all you have left is the greasy box to put your bone in.

Q: Why doesn't Mexico have an Olympic team? A: Because everybody who can run, jump and swim are already in the U.S.

Q: How do you embarrass an archaeologist? A: Give him a used tampon and ask him which period it came from.

Q: What did one broke hooker ask the other? A: Lend me $10 till I'm on my back again.

Q: What's the difference between a redneck and poor white trash? A: a redneck will knock his sister up; poor white trash will marry her.

Q: What is the difference between snowmen and snowwomen? A: Snowballs. Q: What is the metric equivalent of 69? A: 1 ate 1.

Q: What do you call a bunny with a crooked dick? A: FUCKS FUNNY

Q: What's the difference between a Southern zoo and a Northern zoo? A: A Southern zoo has a description of the animal on the front of the cage, along with a recipe.

Q: What's 6 inches long and starts with a p? A: .... a shit (think about it)

Q: Why is being in the military like a blow-job? A. The closer you get to discharge, the better you feel.

Q: What do you call a ninety year old man who can still masturbate? A: Miracle Whip.

Q: How can you tell that you have Africanized bees? A: The

honey tastes like malt liquor.

Q: What do hockey players and Surrey girls have in common? A: They both only change their pads after every third period!

Q: What is the difference between oral and anal sex? A: Oral sex makes your day and Anal sex makes your whole weak.

Q: What's strong enough for a man but made for a woman? A: The back of my hand.

Q: What do you call 300 white men chasing a black man? A: The PGA tour.

Q: What did the bra say to the hat? A: You go on a head while I give these two a lift!

Q: What is a vagina? A: The box a penis comes in.

Q: What do you call 2 jalapenos having sex? A: Fucking hot!

Q: How is a woman like a road? A: Both have manholes.

Q: What do fat chicks and mopeds have in common? A: They are both fun to ride till a friend sees you on them...

Q: How many Emo kids does it take to screw in a lightbulb? A: None, they all sit in the dark and cry.

Q: Why is 88 better than 69? A: Because you get eight twice!

Q: How man Sorority girls does it take to screw in a light bulb? A: Two, One to screw it in, and one to take a picture.

Q: How do you kill a retard? A: Give him a knife and say "Who's special?"

Q: What does a gangbanger have in common with a soda machine? A: They both don't work and always take your money.

Q: Why are there only two pallbearers at a homeless guys funeral? A: There are only two handles on a garbage can.

Q: How do they say "fuck you" in Los Angeles? A: Trust me.

Q: What did the toaster say to the slice of bread? A: I want you inside me!

Q: How do you keep a French person from crashing your party? A: Put a sign up that says "no nudity"

Q: How do you get tickets to the Tampon 100? A: Pull some strings.

Q: Why can't Jesus eat m&m's? A: Because he has holes in his hands.

Q: Why are crippled people always picked on? A: Because they can't stand up for themselves

Q: What's the hardest part about eating a vegetable? A: Putting her back in the wheelchair when you're done...

Q: What would happen if you cut off your left side? A: You would be all right.

Q: What will it take to get a Beatles reunion? A: 2 Bullets

Q: What is Superman's greatest weakness? A: A bucking horse.

Q: How did Rihanna find out Chris Brown was cheating on

her? A: She found another woman's lipstick on his knuckles

Q: What is the recipe for Honeymoon Salad? A: Lettuce alone without dressing. Q: What is a crack head's favorite song? A: I wanna rock!

Q: What do you call money that grows on trees? A: Marijuana

Q: How many parrots can you fit down a man's pants? A: Depends on the length of the perch.

Q: What's worse than getting fingered by Captain Hook? A: Getting raped by jack the ripper.

Q: How do you get retards out of a tree? A: Wave to them!

Q: What do you call a gangbanger behind bars? A: Anything you want.

Q: What do you call a Muslim stripper? A: youseen memuff

Q: Why did the boy fall off the swing? A: He didn't have any arms.

Q: Why are black men penises bigger than white men? A: Because as kids white men had toys to play with!

Q: Why are most Guido's named Tony? A: When they got on the boat to America they stamped To NY (Tony) on their foreheads.

Q: What is the difference between ooooooh and aaaaaaah? A: About three inches.

Q: What's worse than spiders on your piano? A: Crabs on your organ.

Q: Why did the Mafia cross the road? A: Forget about it.

Q: What's the difference between you and eggs? A: Eggs get laid and you don't

Q: How many cops does it take to screw in a lightbulb? A: None they just beat the room for being black.

Q: What do you call a girl with no feet? A: Peggy

Q: What is the flattest surface you can iron your jeans in? A: A white girl's bottom

Q: What did the blind man say when he passed the fish market? A: Good morning ladies.

Q: What did the letter O say to Q? A: Dude, your dick is hanging out.

Q: Why are cowgirls bowlegged? A: Cowboys like to eat with their hats on.

Q: What happens when the smog lifts over Los Angeles? A: UCLA

Q: What is the difference between a genealogist and a gynecologist? A: A genealogist looks up your family tree. A gynecologist looks up your family bush.

Q: What did the Alabama sheriff call the black guy who had been shot 15 times? A: Worst case of suicide he had ever seen.

After a quarrel, a husband said to his wife, "You know, I was a fool when I married you." She replied, "Yes, dear, but I was in love and didn't notice."

Q: What's black, white, and red all over and doesn't fit

through a revolving door? A: A nun with a spear through her head.

Q: Why are pubic Hairs so curly? A: So they don't poke her eye out.

Q: What do you call a gay drive by? A: a fruit roll up.

Q. What's the difference between a bandleader and a gynecologist? A. A bandleader fucks his singers and a gynecologist sucks his fingers.

Q: What has a whole bunch of little balls and screws old ladies? A: A bingo machine.

Q: What did the sign on the door of the whorehouse say? A: Beat it, we're closed.

Q: Did you hear about the paparazzo who was found eating unborn children? A: He was found in the abortion clinic bins looking for the inside scoop.

Q: Why do men like big tits and a tight ass? A: Because they've got big mouths and little dicks.

Q: What's long hard and full of seamen? A: A submarine

Q: What's long, Hard and Erects stuff? A: A Crane!

Q: Did you hear about the Chinese couple that had a retarded baby? A: They named him Sum Ting Wong.

Q: Name the five great kings that have brought happiness in to people's lives A: Drinking Licking sucking fucking and wanking.

Q: What's the difference between onions and prostitutes? A: I cry when I cut up onions...

Q: What do you get when you mix LSD and birth control? A: A trip without the kids!

Q: How do you bring a man back from the dead? A: You suck on his dick until he cums back.

Q: What's the difference between love and herpes? A: Love doesn't last forever.

Q: What's the hardest part of a vegetable to eat? A: The wheelchair!

Q: What's black and eats pussy? A: Cervical cancer!

Q: Who was the most well-known Jewish cook? A: Hitler!

Q: What's the worse side effect of "the pill"? A: Children

Q: What's the difference between a white owl and a black owl? A: A white owl says, "hoot, hoot" a black owl says, "who dat, who dat"

Q: What do you call an IT teacher who touches up his students? A: a PDF File.

Q: Why do men have 2 heads and women 4 lips? A: Because men do all the thinking and women do all the talking.

Q: Why doesn't Tom Cruise eat bananas? A: He can't find the zipper!

Q: What is the irritating part around a blonde's pussy? A: The other guys waiting their turn!

Q: How do you find a blind man in a nudist colony? A: It's not hard.

Q: What's 10 Blocks long and has never had sex? A: The line for the new Call of Duty game.

Q: Why did the Indians come to America first? A: Because they had reservations.

Q: How did you get a fat chick into bed? A: A Piece of Cake.

Q: How do you know if you have an overbite? A: If you're eating pussy and it tastes like shit!

Q: If women with big tits work at Hooters, where do women with only one leg work? A: IHOP!

Q: What do you call a nun in a wheelchair? A: Virgin Mobile

Q: When is an Elf not an Elf? A: When she's sucking your cock, then she's a goblin.

Q. How do you make your girlfriend scream while having sex? A. Call her and tell her.

Q: What do Dale Earnhardt and Pink Floyd have in common? A: Their last big hit was "The Wall"

Q: What do you call a woman who can't make sandwiches? A: Single.

Q: What do you get when you cross A-Rod with Chris Brown? A: A cheater, cheater, woman beater.

Q: Have you heard the one about the lesbian that took Viagra? A: She couldn't get her tongue back in her mouth for a month!

Q: Why don't bunnies make noise when they have sex? A: Because they have cotton balls.

Q: What's the difference between a girlfriend and wife? A: 45 lbs.

Q: What do you call a virgin on a water bed? A: A cherry float.

Q: What do you call a bunch of Asians in a pool? A: Rice Krispies

Q: What's soft and warm when you go to bed, but hard and stiff when you wake up? A: Vomit

Q: What do you get when you cross a turkey with a chicken? A: A clucking gobbler.

Q: What do a nearsighted gynecologist and a puppy have in common? A: A wet nose.

Q: What do you get when you cross a whore with a systems engineer? A: A fuckin know-it-all!

Q: What did Boy George say to Micheal Jackson? A: "You Beat It, and I'll cumma cumma cum."

Q: What do you call a judge with no balls? A: Justice Prick

Q: What does a homeless woman use for a vibrator? A: Two flies in a bottle.

Q. Why can't the post office put Charlie Sheen on a stamp? A. Everyone would be afraid to lick it.

Q: What's the job application to Hooters? A: They just give you a bra and say: Here, fill this out.

Q: What's the hardest part of rollerblading? A: Telling your parents that you are gay.

Q: What do you call lesbian twins? A: Lick-a-likes.

Q: Why don't blind people skydive? A: It scares the shit out of their dogs!

Q: How could the redneck mom tell that her daughter was on her period? A: She could taste the blood on her son's dick!

Q: Did you hear about the blind gynecologist? A: He could read lips!

Q: Why do African Americans only have nightmares? A: Because a redneck shot the only one with a dream!

Q: What's the difference between Jesus and a picture of Jesus? A: It only takes one nail to hang a picture of Jesus.

Q: What's the difference between love, true love, and showing off? A: Spit, swallow, and gargle,

Q: What do you call a redneck bursting into flames? A: A Fire Cracker!

Q: What do you call a Chinese midget? A: Tai Nee

Q: What do you do when your dishwasher stops working? A: Slap her on the ass and tell her to get back to work.

Q: What's the difference between light and hard? A: You can go to sleep with a light on!

Q: Why doesn't a chicken wear pants? A: Because his pecker is on his head!

Q: Why do they call it the wonder bra? A: When you take it off you wonder where her tits went.

Q: Why did God create orgasms? A: So women can moan even when they're happy

Q: What's worse than having sex with a pregnant woman? A: Having sex with a pregnant woman and getting a bj by the baby.

Q: What do you call a teenage girl who doesn't masturbate? A: A liar.

Q: What's the best thing about dating homeless chicks? A: You can drop them off anywhere.

Q: Did you hear about the cannibal who committed suicide? A: He got himself into a real stew.

Q: What did the lesbian vampire say to the other lesbian vampire? A: "I'll see you next month."

Q: Why don't they teach Driver's Ed and sex education on the same day in the Middle East? A: They don't want to wear out the camel.

Q: What did Bill Clinton say to Monica Lewinsky? A: I told you to lick my erection, not wreck my election.

Q: What's even better than winning the Special Olympics A: Not being a retard.

Q: Why do Jewish men like to watch porno movies backwards? A: They like the part where the prostitute gives the money back.

Q: Why do Asian girls have small boobs? A: Because only A's are acceptable

Q: What did one tampon say to the other? A: Nothing. They were both stuck up bitches.

Q: What's the difference between a retard and a pencil? A: The Pencil will eventually get the point.

Q: What do you call a white guy with a huge dick? A: Michael Jackson

Q. How does a Scotsman find a sheep in tall grass? A. Very satisfying.

Q: What's thirty feet long and smells like urine? A: Line dancing at a nursing home.

Q: What do you call Iron Man without his suit? A: Stark naked!

Q: What is the square root of 69? A: Ate something

Q: But do you know what 6.9 is? A: A good thing screwed up by a period.

Q: What do cow pies and cowgirls have in common? A: The older they get the easier they are to pick up.

If the whole world smoked a joint at the same time, there would be world peace for at least two hours. Followed by a global food shortage.

Q: What does a rubix cube and a Penis have in common? A: The more you play with it the harder it gets.

Q: How do you know if your boyfriend has a high sperm count? A: You have to chew before you swallow!

Q: Why did Pizza Hut stop delivering pizza to the ghetto? A: Cuz they were told that Dominoes was always getting played!

Q: Which sexual position produces the ugliest children? A:

Ask your mother!

Q. What do a gynecologist and a pizza boy have in common? A. They can smell it but they can't eat it!

Q: How is pubic hair like parsley? A: You push it to the side before you start eating.

Q: What's the difference between a G-Spot and a golf ball? A: A guy will actually search for a golf ball.

Q: What's the difference between 3 dicks and a joke? A: Your mom can't take a joke.

Q: Why did god invent alcohol? A: So fat women can get laid too.

Q: What is the difference between acne and a catholic priest? A: Acne usually comes on a boy's face after he turns 12

Q: What did one saggy tit say to the other saggy tit? A: If we don't get some support soon, people will think we're nuts!

Q: What's black and fuzzy and hangs from the ceiling? A: A blond electrician.

Q: What do you call a Persian that smokes pot? A: Harry Potter!

Q: What do you call it when a boy and girl make love for the first time? A: Cumming of Age.

Q: What have women and condoms got in common? A: If they're not on your dick they're in your wallet.

Q: What's the difference between a tire and 365 condoms?
A: One's a Goodyear and the other is a fucking goodyear

Q: What is the difference between anal sex and a microwave? A: A microwave doesn't brown your meat!

Q: What do you call a gangster hobbit? A: YOLO SWAGGINS

Q: What do pimps and farmers have in common? A: They both need a hoe to stay in business.

Q: How do you clear out an Afghani bingo game? A: Call B52 Q: What do you call a bunch of white guys sitting on a bench? A: The NBA.

Q: What's warm, wet, and pink? A: a pig in a hot tub.

Q: What is the most common crime in China? A: Identity Fraud.

Q: What do you call an epileptic in a vegetable garden? A: Seizure Salad

Q: What is the definition of Confidence? A: When your wife catches you in bed with another woman and you slap her on the ass and say, "You're next Baby... !"

Q: Why were the two whores travelling in London pissed off? A: Because they found out that Big Ben was a clock!

Q: Why is sperm white and piss yellow? A: So you know if you're cumming or going

Q: How do you stop a clown from smiling? A: Shoot him in the face!

Q: What's the difference between a pregnant woman and a light bulb? A: You can unscrew a light bulb.

Q: What do you call a country where everyone is pissed? A: A urination.

Q: What did the moose say after leaving the gay bar? A: Man, I blew like 50 bucks in there.

Q: What's the best part of gardening? A: Getting down and dirty with my hoes.

Q: What do you call a Chinese rapist? A: Rai Ping Yu

Q: What's the Difference between kinky and perverted? A1: Kinky is when you tickle your girlfriends ass with a feather. A2: Perverted is when you use the whole chicken...

Q: Did you hear about the Waffle House waitress they found murdered behind the restaurant dumpster? A: She was scattered, smothered, covered, chunked, topped, and diced.

Q: What's the difference between a penis and a bonus? A: Your wife will always blow your bonus!

A recent survey shows that sperm banks beat blood banks in contributions...HANDS DOWN!

If you force sex on a prostitute, is it rape or shoplifting? You choose.

Q: What did the hardboiled egg say to the boiling water? A: I can't get a hard-on because I was just laid.

Q: What is Moby Dick's dad's name? A: Papa Boner

Q: How do you make a pool table laugh? A: Tickle its balls

Q: What do u call hooker that likes in in her ass? A: a crack whore

Q: What do you call a dictionary on drugs? A: addictionary.

Q: Did you hear about the hitman who's also a janitor at the aquarium? A: He sweeps with the fishes! Me: I know a gay guy that sounds like an owl. Friend: Who?

Q: Did you hear that the energizer bunny was arrested? A: He was charged with battery.

Q: What has two wings and a halo? A: A Chinese telephone.... "Wing wing alo?"

Q: What's worse than finding a Justin Bieber CD in your boyfriend's bedroom? A: Finding a box of tissues next to it.

Q: How do you eat a squirrel? A: You spread its little legs.

Q: What do you call a guy with no arms and no legs hanging on the wall? A: Art

Q: Why did the snowman smile? A: Because the snowblower is coming.

One day, a little boy wrote to Santa Clause, "Please send me a sister." Santa Clause wrote him back, "Ok, send me your mother."

Q: Why is Santa so jolly? A: Because he knows where all the naughty girls live.

Q: Why doesn't Santa have any kids? A: He only comes once a year.

Q: Why was two piece swimsuit invented? A: To separate the hairy from the dairy.

Q: Did you hear about the junkie that was addicted to brake fluid? A: He said he could stop anytime

Roses are red that much is true but violets are purple not fucking blue.

Mom: If a boy touches your boobs say "don't" and if he touches your pussy say "stop"? Girl: But mom, he touched both so I said "don't stop"

After 20 years of marriage, I still get blow jobs. If my wife finds out, she'll f**king kill me.

Did you hear about that kid that had sex with his teacher? Yeah, he recently died from hi-fiving.

Whenever I have a one night stand, I always use protection. A fake name and a fake number.

Girl: My favorite number is 16 Boy: why? Girl: because you get 8 (ate) twice!

It would be a lot easier to be a hard worker if my company didn't block access to porn sites on the internet.

How many guys can participate in a gang bang before it's gay?

The biggest difference between men and women is what comes to mind when the word 'Facial' is used.

Women fake orgasms to have relationships. Men fake relationships to have orgasms.

A vagina is like the weather. Once it's wet, it's time to go inside

Have you heard of the new movie called "Constipation"? It hasn't come out yet.

Once you go Asian, you never miss an equation.

I'd like to point out that 'beautiful' has u in it. But, 'quickie' has u & I together.

When Hugh Hefner dies, will he really be going to a better place?

Everything is made in China... Except for baby girls

I got raped by an alligator the other day. I think I have gatoraids.

Roses are red. Nuts are round. Skirts go up. Panties go down. Belly to belly. Skin to skin. When it's stiff, stick it in.

Sex, drugs, rock & roll; speed, weed, & birth control. Life's a bitch and then you die, so fuck the world and let's get high!

I'm trying to write a joke about unemployed people... But it needs more work

Vending machines are so homophobic. I'm sorry my dollar is not straight enough for you.

A guy goes to the store to buy condoms. 'Do you want a bag?', the cashier asks 'No', the guy says, 'she's not that ugly'

Relationships used to be X's an O's , now its just Exes and Hoes...

Diarrhea is hereditary, it runs in your jeans.

It sucks to be a penis because your roommates are nuts, your neighbor is an ass hole, your best friend is a pussy, and your owner strangles you every night until you throw up!

Why is it called "taking a dump" when you are leaving one!

I wish I had parents like Dora. They let that b*tch go everywhere.

White people fairy tales: Once upon a time. Black people fairy tales: Yall motherfuc*as ain't believe dis' shit!

A PENIS is the lightest thing in the world. Even a thought can raise it.

Real men don't wear pink, they eat it.

A pervert walks over to this sorority girl, he said "Bend over and spell run." So she bent over next thing she knew there was a sharp pain she said "R U N" The perverted guy said "As far as I can go."

Scientists say the average size of the male penis has gone down to 5 inches. This just shows how big the Chinese population is getting.

Q: What does a nosey pepper do? A: Gets jalapeno business!

Q: What do you call a fake noodle? A: An Impasta

Q: What do you call an alligator in a vest? A: An Investigator

Q: What happens if you eat yeast and shoe polish? A: Every morning you'll rise and shine!

Q: "What's the difference between a guitar and a fish?" A: "You can't tuna fish."

Q: What do you call a pile of kittens A: a meowntain

Q: What do you call a baby monkey? A: A Chimp off the old block.

Q: Did you hear about the race between the lettuce and the tomato? A: The lettuce was a "head" and the tomato was trying to "ketchup"!

Q: Did you hear about the hungry clock? A: It went back four seconds.

Q: What do you call a boy who finally stood up to the bullies? A: An ambulance.

Q: Why can't you give Elsa a balloon? A: Because she will Let it go.

Q: What do you get from a pampered cow? A: Spoiled milk.

Q: If Mississippi bought Virginia a New Jersey, what would Delaware? A: Idaho... Alaska!

Q: Did you hear about that new broom? A: It's sweeping the nation!

Q: What do you call an elephant that doesn't matter? A: An irrelephant.

Q: What do lawyers wear to court? A: Lawsuits!

Q: What gets wetter the more it dries? A: A towel.

Q: Where do crayons go on vacation? A: Color-ado!

Q: Why did the belt get arrested? A: He held up a pair of pants.

Q: What do you call a fat psychic? A: A four chin teller.

Q: What do you call a computer floating in the ocean? A: A Dell Rolling in the Deep.

Q: What did Bacon say to Tomato? A: Lettuce get together!

Q: What do you call a computer that sings? A: A-Dell

Q: Did you hear about the shampoo shortage in Jamaica? A: It's dread-full.

Q: What is it called when a cat wins a dog show? A: A CAT-HAS-TROPHY!

Q: How do you make a tissue dance? A: Put a little boogey in it!

Q: What is heavy forward but not backward? A: Ton.

Q: What do you call a gangsta snowman? A: Froze-T

Q: What did the femur say to the patella? A: I kneed you.

Q: What do you get if you cross a cat with a dark horse? A: Kitty Perry

Q: Why did the picture go to jail? A: Because it was framed.

Q: What do you call a three-footed aardvark? A: a yardvark!

Q: What do you get when you cross fish and an elephant? A: Swimming trunks.

Q: Where do bees go to the bathroom? A: At the BP station!

Q: Who earns a living driving their customers away? A: A taxi driver.

Q: What do you call a laughing jar of mayonnaise? A: LMAYO

Q: What do you call a dinosaur with a extensive vocabulary?
A: a thesaurus.

Q: "How do you shoot a killer bee?" A: "With a bee bee gun."

Q: How do you drown a Hipster? A: In the mainstream.

Q: What kind of jokes do you make in the shower? A: Clean Jokes!

Q: What did the baby corn say to the mama corn? A: "Where's Popcorn?"

Q: What do you call sad coffee?" A: Despresso.

Q: How do you make holy water? A: Boil the hell out of it!

Q: What happened to the dog that swallowed a firefly? A: It barked with de-light!

Q: What stays in the corner and travels all over the world? A: A stamp.

Q: What do you call a man with no body and just a nose? A: Nobody nose.

Q: Why did the computer go to the doctor? A: Because it had a virus!

Q: Why are frogs so happy? A: They eat whatever bugs them

Q: What is brown and has a head and a tail but no legs? A: A penny.

Q: How do you make an Octopus laugh? A: With ten-tickles

Q: Why are pirates called pirates? A: Cause they arrrrr.

Q: What is the tallest building in the world? A: The library! It has the most stories!

Q: What's the first bet that most people make in their lives? A: the alpha bet

Q. What do you get when you cross a cow and a duck? A. Milk and quackers!

Q: How do you organize a space party? A: You planet!

Q: What did the leopard say after eating his owner? A: Man, that hit the "spot."

Q: What do you call a sleeping bull? A: A bulldozer!

Q: What do you call security guards working outside Samsung shops? A: Guardians of the Galaxy.

Q: What do you call having your grandma on speed dial? A: Instagram.

Q: Why did the banana go to the Doctor? A: Because it was not peeling well

Q: Why is England the wettest country? A: Because the queen has reigned there for years!

Q: What belongs to you but others use more? A: Your name

Q: Why do fish live in salt water? A: Because pepper makes them sneeze!

Q: Why did the man put his money in the freezer? A: He wanted cold hard cash!

Q: What do you get when you cross a snowman with a vampire? A: Frostbite.

Q: What is the best day to go to the beach? A: Sunday, of course!

Q: Which is the building is the largest? A: The library because it has the most stories.

Q: What do you call an illegally parked frog? A: Toad.

Q: What bow can't be tied? A: A rainbow!

Q: What do you call a laughing motorcycle? A: A Yamahahaha

Q: What season is it when you are on a trampoline? A: Spring time.

Q: Where did the computer go to dance? A: To a disc-o.

Q: What has one head, one foot and four legs? A: A Bed

Q: What is the difference between a school teacher and a train? A: The teacher says spit your gum out and the train says "chew chew chew".

Q: Why did the birdie go to the hospital? A: To get a tweetment.

Q: Why did the cross-eyed teacher lose her job? A: Because she couldn't control her pupils?

Q: What do you call someone who is afraid of Santa? A: A Claustrophobic

Q: What three candies can you find in every school? A: Nerds, DumDums, and smarties.

Q: What sound do porcupines make when they kiss? A: Ouch

Q: Why was the guy looking for fast food on his friend? A: Because his friend said dinner is on me.

Q: Did you hear the joke about the roof? A: Never mind, it's over your head!

Q: What do you call a bee that lives in America? A: USB

Q: How do you make a tissue dance? A: Put a bogey in it.

Q: Why didn't the skeleton go to the dance? A: Because he had no-body to go with.

Q: How do crazy people go through the forest? A: They take the psycho path.

Q: Did you hear about the angry pancake? A: He just flipped.

Q: What do prisoners use to call each other? A: Cell phones.

Q: What do you call a cow with a twitch? A: Beef Jerky.

Q: Did you ever hear about that movie constipation? A: It never came out.

Q: What Do You Call A Bear With No Teeth? A: A Gummy Bear

Q: What do you get when you cross Sonic the Hedgehog and Curious George? A: 2 Fast 2 Curious

Q: Did you hear about the hairdresser? A: She dyed.

Q: What do you call a musician with problems? A: a trebled man.

Q: Did you hear about the Italian chef that died? A: He pasta way.

Q: Where do snowmen keep their money? A: In snow banks.

Q: What do you call a very religious person that sleep walks? A: a Roman Catholic

Q: Did you hear about the crab that went to the seafood disco? A: He pulled a muscle

Q: Did you hear about the carrot detective? A: He got to the root of every case.

Q: Why can't you take a nap during a race? A: Because if you snooze, you lose!

Q. What did the tie say to the hat? A. You go on ahead and I'll hang around

Q: What washes up on very small beaches? A: Microwaves!

Q: What never asks questions but receives a lot of answers? A: the Telephone.

Q: What goes through towns, up & over hills, but doesn't move? A: The road!

Q: Did you hear about the guy who got hit in the head with a can of soda? A: He was lucky it was a soft drink.

Q: Why was there thunder and lightning in the lab? A: The scientists were brainstorming!

Q: What did Delaware? A: a New Jersey

Q: Why did Tony go out with a prune? A: Because he couldn't find a date!

Q: What do you call purple when it is being mean? A:

Violent.

Q: What did the little mountain say to the big mountain? A: Hi Cliff!

Q: Did you hear the one about the geologist? A: He took his wife for granite so she left him

Q: What did Winnie The Pooh say to his agent? A: Show me the honey!

Q: What did the man say to the wall? A: One more crack like that and I'll plaster ya!

Q: What do you get when you cross a fridge with a radio? A: Cool Music

Q: Why couldn't the pirate play cards? A: Because he was sitting on the deck!

Q: What's the difference between bird flu and swine flu? A: If you have bird flu, you need tweetment. If you have swine flu, you need oink-ment.

Q: Why did the traffic light turn red? A: You would too if you had to change in the middle of the street!

Q: What did one elevator say to the other elevator? A: I think I'm coming down with something!

Q: What do you call a window that raps? A: 2PANEZ

Q: What happened when a faucet, a tomato and lettuce were in a race? A: The lettuce was ahead, the faucet was running and the tomato was trying to ketchup.

Q: Why can't your nose be 12 inches long? A: Because then it would be a foot!

Q: What has four wheels and flies? A: A garbage truck!

Q: What starts with a P, ends with an E, and has a million letters in it? A: Post Office!

Q: What do you call a belt with a watch on it? A: A waist of time

Q: What did the blanket say to the bed? A: Don't worry, I've got you covered!

Q: Why should you take a pencil to bed? A: To draw the curtains!

Q: What do you call an unpredictable, out of control photographer? A: a loose Canon

Q: What do you call a frozen dog? A: A pupsicle.

Q: What does the Lone Ranger say when he takes out the garbage? A: To the dump, to the dump, to the dump dump dump.

Q: How many books can you put in an empty backpack? A: One! After that its not empty!

Q: What kind of button won't unbutton? A: A bellybutton!

Q: What do you call an 80s synth pop band with a scoop of ice cream? A: Depeche a la Mode.

Q: What do you call a group of men waiting for a haircut? A: A barbecue

Q: Why do sea-gulls fly over the sea? A: Because if they

flew over the bay they would be bagels!

Q: What dog keeps the best time? A: A watch dog.

Q: What do you call a condiment with a hit single? A: a must"heard"

Q: What do you call two fat people having a chat? A: A heavy discussion

Q: Why did the tomato turn red? A: It saw the salad dressing!

Q: What do you get when you plant kisses? A: Tu-lips (two-lips)

Q: What did the daddy chimney say to the baby chimney? A: You are to little to smoke!

Q: What do you call a ghosts mom and dad? A: Transparents

Q: Why did God make only one Yogi Bear? A: Because when he tried to make a second one he made a Boo-Boo

Q: What did the grape do when it got stepped on? A: It let out a little wine!

Q: What do you call the new girl at the bank? A: The Nutella!

Q: What did the judge say when the skunk walked in the court room? A: Odor in the court.

Q: What did the fish say when he swam into the wall? A: Dam!

Q: Why don't skeletons fight each other? A: They don't have

the guts.

Q: What do you call cheese that is not yours? A: Nacho Cheese

Q: What streets do ghosts haunt? A: Dead ends!

Q: Did you hear about the astronaut who stepped on chewing gum? A: He got stuck in Orbit.

Q: What did the penny say to the other penny? A: We make perfect cents.

Q: Why did the man with one hand cross the road? A: To get to the second hand shop.

Q: Why did the boy sprinkle sugar on his pillow before he went to sleep? A: So he could have sweet dreams.

Q: What do you call a nervous javelin thrower? A: Shakespeare.

Q: Did you hear about the painter who was hospitalized? A: Reports say it was due to too many strokes.

Q: Why did the robber take a bath? A: Because he wanted to make a clean getaway.

Q: What happens if life gives you melons? A: Your dyslexic

Q: What did the judge say to the dentist? A: Do you swear to pull the tooth, the whole tooth and nothing but the tooth.

Q: Why did the boy tiptoe past the medicine cabinet? A: He didn't want to wake the sleeping pills!

Q: What do you call a funny mountain? A: hill-arious

Q: What goes up when the rain comes down? A: An umbrella.

Q: Why did the belt go to jail? A: Because it held up a pair of pants!

Q: Did you hear about the calendar thief? A: He got 12 months; they say his days are numbered

Q: What happens if life gives you melons? A: Your dyslexic

Q: What did one raindrop say to the other? A: Two's company, three's a cloud

Q: Why did the balloon burst? A: Because is saw a lolly pop

Q: Did you hear about the sick juggler? A: They say he couldnt stop throwing up!

Q: What kind of driver never get a parking ticket? A: A screw driver

Q: What did the stamp say to the envelope? A: Stick with me and we will go places!

Q: Who can shave 10 times a day and still have a beard? A: A barber.

Q: What do you call a horse that can't lose a race? A: Sherbet

Q: What do you call a dentist in the army? A: A drill sergeant

Q: What did the triangle say to the circle? A: You're pointless!

Q: Did you hear about the new Johnny Depp movie? A: It's

the one rated Arrrr!

Q: Why does a milking stool have only 3 legs? A: Because the cow has the utter.

Q: What's easy to get into but hard to get out of? A: Trouble

Q: Did you hear about the guy who died when an axe fell on him? A: The police are calling it an axe-i-dent.

Q: Why did the dinosaur cross the road? A: Because the chicken joke wasn't invented yet.

Q: What kind of lights did Noah use on the Ark? A: Flood lights!

Q: Did you hear about the monster with five legs? A: His trousers fit him like a glove.

Q: Why don't you see giraffes in elementary school? A: Because they're all in High School!

Q: Which is the longest word in the dictionary? A: "Smiles", because there is a mile between each "s"!

Q: What happened to the wooden car with wooden wheels and wooden engine? A: it wooden go!

Q: Which month do soldiers hate most? A: The month of March!

Q: What did the painter say to the wall? A: One more crack like that and I'll plaster you!

Q: What do you call a Bee who is having a bad hair day? A: A Frisbee.

Q: What did the M&M go to college? A: Because he wanted to be a Smarty.

Q: What stays on the ground but never gets dirty? A: Shadow.

Q: What kind of shorts do clouds wear? A: Thunderwear

Q: Why do golfers wear two pairs of pants? A: In case they get a hole in one!

Q: What kind of berry has a coloring book? A: A crayon-berry

Q: What do you call a magician on a plane? A: A flying sorcerer!

Q: Why did the toilet paper roll down the hill? A: He wanted to get to the bottom.

Q: Who cleans the bottom of the ocean? A: A Mer-Maid

Q: When's the best time to go to the dentist? A: Tooth-hurty

Q: What did one aspiring wig say to the other aspiring wig? A: I wanna get a head!

Q: Did you hear about the paddle sale at the boat store? A: It was quite an oar deal.

Q: Why did Goofy put a clock under his desk? A: Because he wanted to work over-time!

Q: Do you know why diarrhea is hereditary? A: Because it runs through your jeans.

What would you do if I stole a kiss? Call the Police

Q: What do you call a South American girl who is always in a hurry? A: Urgent Tina

Q: Why did Johnny throw the clock out of the window? A: Because he wanted to see time fly!

Q: When do you stop at green and go at red? A: When you're eating a watermelon!

Q: What did the tailor think of her new job? A: It was sew sew.

Q: How did the farmer mend his pants? A: With cabbage patches!

Q: Why did the man lose his job at the orange juice factory? A: He couldn't concentrate!

Q: Can I tell you a joke about paper. A: Nah, never mind, its tearable.

Q: How do you repair a broken tomato? A: Tomato Paste!

Q: Why did the baby strawberry cry? A: Because his parents were in a jam!

Q: What did the hamburger name his daughter? A: Patty!

Q: What kind of egg did the bad chicken lay? A: A deviled egg!

Q: What kind of key opens the door on Thanksgiving? A: A turkey!

Q: Why did the cookie go to the hospital? A: He felt crummy!

Q: Why were the teacher's eyes crossed? A: She couldn't control her pupils!

Q: What do you call a guy who never farts in public? A: A

private tutor.

Q: What do you call a bear with no socks on? A: Bare-foot.

Q: What can you serve but never eat? A: A volleyball.

Q: What kind of shoes do all spies wear? A: Sneakers.

Q: Why did the soccer player bring string to the game? A: So he could tie the score.

Q: Why is a baseball team similar to a muffin? A: They both depend on the batter.

Q: What did the alien say to the garden? A: Take me to your weeder.

Q: What do you call two fat people having a chat? A: A heavy discussion.

Q: Did you hear about the two bed bugs who met in the mattress? A: They got married in the spring.

Q: Why do watermelons have fancy weddings? A: Because they cantaloupe.

Q: Have you heard the joke about the butter? A: I better not tell you, it might spread.

Q: How do baseball players stay cool? A: They sit next to their fans.

Q: Why was the math book sad? A: Because it had too many problems.

Q: What runs but doesn't get anywhere? A: A refrigerator.

Q: What is an astronaut's favorite place on a computer? A: The Space bar!

Q: Why was the robot mad? A: People kept pushing its buttons.

Q: What exam do young witches have to pass? A: A spelling test!

Q: What do you call a sheep with no head and no legs? A: A cloud!

Q: Why did the boy eat his homework? A: Because his teacher said it was a piece of cake!

Q: Why is Basketball such a messy sport? A: Because you dribble on the floor!

Q: How do you communicate with a fish? A: Drop him a line!

Q: What did the digital watch say to his grandfather? A: Look grandpa no hands!

Q: Where do sheep go to get haircuts? A: To the Baa Baa shop!

Q: What does a shark like to eat with peanut butter? A: Jellyfish!

Q: What do cats eat for breakfast? A: Mice Crispies!

Q: Why can't a leopard hide? A: Because he's always spotted!

Q: What do you give a dog with a fever? A: Mustard, its the best thing for a hot dog!

Q: What do you get when you cross a cat with a lemon? A: A sour puss!

Q: What kind of flower doesn't sleep at night? A: The Day-

DIRTY, CHEESY AND ABSOLUTELY AWFUL DAD JOKES

zzz

Q: Why do birds fly south for the winter? A: Its easier than walking!

Q: What kind of key opens a banana? A: A monkey!

Q: Did you hear about the vampire bicycle that went round biting people's arms off? A: It was a vicious cycle.

Q: How do you know that carrots are good for your eyesight? A: Have you ever seen a rabbit wearing glasses?

Q: Why does a hummingbird hum? A: It doesn't know the words!

Q: What did one plate say to the other? A: Dinners on me

Q: Why are some fish at the bottom of the ocean? A: Because they dropped out of school!

Q: What goes up and down but doesn't move? A: The temperature!

Q: Which weighs more, a ton of feathers or a ton of bricks? A: Neither, they both weigh a ton!

Q: Did you hear about the blonde who gave her cat a bath? A: She still hasn't gotten all the hair off her tongue.

Q: What has one horn and gives milk A: A milk truck.

Q: Where do bulls get their messages? A: On a bull-etin board.

Q: What do bulls do when they go shopping? A: They CHARGE!

Q: What do you call a house that likes food? A: a

Condoment!

Q: What runs but can't walk? A: The faucet!

Q: What kind of bed does a mermaid sleep in? A: A water bed!

Q: What kind of crackers do firemen like in their soup? A: Firecrackers!

Q: Why did the barber win the race? A: Because he took a short cut.

Q: Where do boats go when they get sick? A: The dock

Q: What do you call leftover aliens? A: Extra Terrestrials.

Q: What's taken before you get it? A: Your picture.

Q: What's the difference between roast beef and pea soup? A: You can roast beef, but you cant pea soup!

Q: What concert costs 45 cents? A: 50 Cent featuring Nickleback.

Q: Can February March? A: No. But April May.

Did you hear about the injured vegetable? Some say he got beet.

Q: Why did the tree go to the dentist? A: To get a root canal.

Q: What is it called when a cat wins a dog show? A: A CAT-HAS-TROPHY!

Q: Why was the broom late? A: It over swept!

Q: Why is a 2016 calendar more popular than a 2015 calendar? A: It has more dates.

Q: What caused the airline to go bankrupt? A: Runway inflation.

Q: What do you call a snowman with a six pack? A: An abdominal snowman.

Q: Did you hear the joke about the germ? A: Never mind. I don't want to spread it around

Q: What do you call a person that chops up cereal? A: a cereal killer.

Q: What do you call a crushed angle? A: a rectangle

Q: Who do fish always know how much they weigh? A: Because they have their own scales.

Q: Why didn't the 11 year old go to the pirate movie? A: because it was rated arrrrr

Q: What did the janitor say when he jumped out of the closet? A: SUPPLIES!

Q: What did the tie say to the hat? A: You go on ahead and I'll hang around!

Q: Did you hear about the limo driver who went 25 years without a customer? A: All that time and nothing to chauffeur it.

Q: Why did the scarecrow win the nobel prize? A: Because he was outstanding in his field.

Q: What pet makes the loudest noise? A: A trum-pet! Q: Did you hear about the kidnapping? A: He woke up.

Q: What the difference between you and a calendar? A: a calendar has dates.

Q: What do you call a rabbit with fleas? A: Bugs Bunny!

Q: What word looks the same backwards and upside down? A: Swims

Q: Why did the manager hire the marsupial? A: Because he was koala-fied.

Q: How many tickles does it take to make an octopus laugh? A: Tentacles.

Q: What do you get if you cross a card game with a typhoon? A: Bridge over troubled water.

Q: Have you ever tried to eat a clock? A: It's very time consuming.

Q: Did you hear about the ghost comedian? A: He was booed off stage.

Q: What do you get when you cross the Godfather with an attorney? A: An offer you can't understand.

Q: What kind of emotions do noses feel? A: Nostralgia. Why did the dog cross the road? To get to the "barking" lot!

Q: How do spiders communicate? A: Through the World Wide Web.

Q: Why are chefs so mean? A: They beat eggs and whip cream.

Q: Did you hear about the guy who's whole left side was cut off? A: He's all right now.

Q: Did you hear about the paper boy? A: He blew away

Q: When I was young there was only 25 letters in the

Alphabet? A: Nobody new why.

Q: What do you get when you cross Speedy Gonzales with a country singer? A: Arriba McEntire.

Q: What do you get when you cross a lawyer with the Godfather? A: An offer you can't understand.

Q: Did you hear about the circus fire? A: Yeah, it was in'tents'.

Q: Why did the scientist go to the tanning salon? A: Because he was a paleontologist.

Q: Where does bad light go? A: PRISM!

Q: Why did the hot dog turn down a chance to star in a major motion picture? A: None of the rolls (roles) were good enough.

Q: Did you hear about the new corduroy pillowcases? A: Their making headlines...

Q: Why did the log fall into a creek? A: Because that's how it ROLLS!

Q. What did the pink panther say when he stepped on the ant? A. deadant deadant deadant deadant.

Q: What kind of bird sticks to sweaters? A: a Vel-Crow. Music Teacher:

What's your favorite musical instrument? Fat Kid: The lunch bell

Q: Why did the two 4's skip lunch? A: They already 8 (ate).

Q: Why did the girl bring lipstick and eye shadow to school?

A: She had a make-up exam!

Q: Why did the insomniac man get arrested? A: He resisted a rest

Q: Why did the computer break up with the internet? A: There was no "Connection".

Q: What vehicle has 4 wheels and flies? A: a garbage truck.

Q: Why did the music teacher need a ladder? A: To reach the high notes.

Q: What music are balloons scared of? A: Pop music

Q: What do you call a book that's about the brain? A: A mind reader.

Q: Who goes to the bathroom in the middle of a party? A: A party pooper.

Q. Did you hear about the party a little boy had for his sisters barbie dolls? A. It was a Barbie-Q.

Q: How does a suit put his child into bed? A: He tux him in

Q: What's the difference between a cat and a frog? A: A Cat has nine lives but a Frog croaks every night!

Q: What is a tree's favorite drink? A: Root beer!

Q: What four letters will frighten a burglar? A: O I C U

Q: What do sea monsters eat? A: Fish and ships

Q: I can run but not walk, have a mouth but can't talk, and a bed, but I do not sleep.

What am I? A: A River. lol = Drowning Man. *lol* = Drowning

Cheerleader.

Want to hear a dirty joke? A kid jumped into a mud puddle.

Want to hear a clean joke? A kid jumped into the bath.

What did one ocean say to the other? THEY just waved.... Did you sea what I did.... No? I'm shore you did.

"Two peanuts were walking down the street. One was asalted."

I've just opened a new restaurant called Karma. There's no menu, we just give you what you deserve.

I had a dream I was a muffler and I woke up exhausted.

My sister bet me a £1,000,000 that I couldn't make a car out of spaghetti, you should have seen her face when I drove pasta.

Today I gave my dead batteries away....Free of charge.

Never give up on your dreams, keep sleeping.

If you are running next to me on the treadmill, the answer is YES, we are racing.

Being honest may not get you a lot of FRIENDS but it'll always get you the RIGHT ONES.

I'm going to stand outside. So if anyone asks, I am outstanding.

I am going bananas. That's what i say to my bananas before i leave the house

I'm so bright my mother calls me son.

My eyelids are so sexy, I can't keep my eyes off them.

The past, present and future walk into a bar. It was tense.

One hat said to the other you stay here I'll go on a head

What fits your schedule better......Exercising 1 hour a day or being fat 24 hours a day?

Silence is golden, Duct tape is silver

I know some jokes about unemployment but they need some work.

I have never seen a fruit PUNCH and a cereal BOX If you think of a better fish pun. Let minnow.

A three legged dog walks in the bar and says - "I'm lookin' for the guy who shot my paw"

I tried to catch some fog earlier. I mist.

Hey, I changed my password to incorrect because if I forget, it would say your password is incorrect!

Change is hard. Have you ever tried to bend a coin?

If money doesn't grow on trees why do banks have branches?

Did you hear about the farmer who fed his cows birdseed and started selling cheep milk

A butcher goes on a first date and says 'It was nice meating you'

two lumps of vomit are flying through the air one says to the other "you look upset" the other one says "I know i was brought up around here.

2 Pacs of Eminems for 50 Cents? Man that's Ludacris

I can't believe I got fired from the calendar factory. All I did was take a day off.

I wonder if earth makes fun of other planets for having no life.

It's been scientifically proven that too many birthdays can kill you!

Don't tell a secrets in a cornfield. There a too many ears

Why do we cook bacon and bake cookies?

Why do you drive down a parkway but park in a driveway?

fi yuo cna raed tihs whit no porlbem, yuo aer smrat.

I hated my job as an origami teacher. Too much paperwork.

I love pressing F5. It's so refreshing.

Why is everything delivered by a ship called cargo but if it's delivered by a car it's a shipment?

Man delivers load of bubble wrap. Where do you want this he asks? Just pop it in the corner was the reply.

I moustache you a question, but I'll shave it for later.

"When I die, I want my tombstone to be a WiFi hotspot......that way people visit more often.

" Why do they call it a hot water heater when you don't have to heat hot water?

What happens when you get scared half to death twice?

A police recruit was asked during the exam, "What would you do if you had to arrest your own mother?" He said, "Call for backup."

Q: Did you hear about the scientist whose wife had twins? A: He baptized one and kept the other as a control.

Q: What's the difference between love and marriage? A: Love is one long sweet dream, and marriage is the alarm clock.

Q: What kind of institution is Marriage? A: One where a man loses his Bachelor's Degree and the woman gets her Masters.

Q: What does marriage do? A: Puts a ring on a woman's finger and two under the man's eyes.

Q: What kind of rings do men need for marriage A1: Engagement Ring A2: Wedding Ring A3: Suffe-Ring A4: Endu-Ring

Q: What's the definition of a happy marriage? A: One where the husband gives and the wife takes.

What's the cure for marriage? Answer: Alcoholism.

Q: What's the difference between love and marriage? A: Love is blind and marriage is an eye-opener!

Son: How much does it cost to get married, Dad? Father: I don't know son, I'm still paying for it.

Son: Is it true? Dad, I heard that in India, a man doesn't know his wife until he marries. Father: That happens everywhere, son, everywhere!

Q: When are feminists bad? A: After one marries your sister!

Q: Who is the perfect husband? A: One who keeps his mouth shut and his checkbook open!

Q: When is it okay to Love thy neighbor? A: When her husband is away on business!

Q: How hard is it to lose a wife? A: Nowadays its almost impossible!

Q: Why shouldn't you marry a tennis player? A: Because love means nothing to them!

Q: What's the difference between marrying a Mama's Boy and a Daddy's Girl? A: One makes biscuits like his mother and the other makes dough like her father!

Q: The difference between marriage and death? A: Dead people are free.

Q: What is the ideal marriage? A: One between a deaf man and a blind woman

Q: I married Miss Right. A: I just didn't know her first name was "Always."

Q: Which one of your children will never grow up and move away? A: Your husband!

Q: How do you turn a fox into an elephant? A: Marry it.

Q: How do you transfer funds even faster than electronic banking? A: By getting Married!

Q: What's the difference between the Bride and Groom A: In

marriage, the bride gets a shower. But for the groom, it's curtains!

Q: Marriage is what kind of sport? A: One where the trapped animal has to buy the license!

Q: What kind of process is Marriage? A: A process of finding out what kind of man your wife would have preferred.

The gods gave man fire and he invented fire engines. They gave him love and he invented marriage.

With her marriage, she got a new name and a dress. Today I thought I lost my wife for a second... then I looked outside the kitchen.

If 50 percent of marriages end in divorce the other half must end in death.

Marriage is the process of finding out what kind of man your wife would have preferred.

My wife said "I think it's time we heard the pitter patter of little feet again. So I bought her a rat.

The best way to propose to a woman is to carry her on a boat, paddle the boat to the middle of the river then tell her "Marry me or get off my boat"

Relationships are like fat people. Most of them don't work out.

One time when I was talking to my mom's co-worker he said that he had no friends. He said that all of his friends were either married or dead. And my friend who is with me says to him "What's the difference?"

A husband and wife were in bed watching tv. The husband had the remote in hand switching back and forth between the porn and fishing channels. The wife got pissed off grabbed the remote and kept it on the porn channel and said to hubby.. "Leave it on the porn channel you already know how to fish."

A man walked out to the street and caught a taxi just going by. He got into the taxi, and the cabbie said, "Perfect timing. You're just like Ryan" Passenger: "Who?" Cabbie: "Ryan Jay Robinson. He's a guy who did everything right all the time. Like my coming along when you needed a cab, things happen like that to Ryan Jay Robinson, every single time." Passenger: "There are always a few clouds over everybody." Cabbie: "Not Ryan Jay Robinson. He was a terrific athlete. He could have won the Grand Slam at tennis. He could golf with the pros. He sang like an opera baritone and danced like a Broadway star and you should have heard him play the piano. He was an amazing guy." Passenger: "Sounds like he was something really special." Cabbie: "There's more. He had a memory like a computer. He remembered everybody's birthday. He knew all about wine, which foods to order and which fork to eat them with. He could fix anything. Not like me. I change a fuse, and the whole street blacks out. But Ryan Jay Robinson, he could do everything right." Passenger: "Wow. Some guy then." Cabbie: "He always knew the quickest way to go in traffic and avoid traffic jams. Not like me, I always seem to get stuck in them. But Ryan, he never made a mistake, and he really knew how to treat a woman and make her feel good. He would never answer her back even if she was in the wrong; and his clothing was always immaculate, shoes highly polished too. He was the perfect man! He never made a mistake. No one could ever measure up to Ryan Jay Robinson." Passenger: "An amazing fellow. How did you meet him?" Cabbie: "Well, I never actually met Ryan. He died. I'm married to his widow."

An old lady gets caught shoplifting. On court day the lady and her husband who goes with her stands before the judge and he says to her, "Why did you shoplift?" And she says "I was hungry." The judge says "What did you take?" She replys, "A can of peaches." So the judge trying to figure out how to punish her says, "How many peaches where in the can?" The lady says "6" so the judge says ok then 1 day per peach in jail that will be 6 days time served. The judge says would anyone like to say anything and her husband says your honor, "She stole a can of peas too"

There once was a hottie who got very drunk at a bar and asked a man sitting behind here to marry her. The man replied no and a few hours later told his friends what happened They then asked why he said No? The man replies "Why would I get on one knee for a woman who wouldn't get on two knees for me".

Q: How do you blind a woman? A: You put a windshield in front of her.

Q: Why are women like clouds? A: Eventually they go away and its a nice day.

Q: What is loud and obnoxious? A: A woman. A quiet man, is a thinking man. A quiet woman, is usually mad.

Q: Why is life like a penis? A: Women make it hard!

Q: Why do women have periods? A: Because they deserve them.

Q: What do you call a woman without an asshole? A: SINGLE!

Q: What's the most common sleeping position of a woman? A: Around.

Q: What do you call a woman with no clitoris? A: It doesn't matter, she's not going to come.

Q: What did one girl firefly say to the other? A: You glow girl!

Q: Why are men sexier than women? A: You can't spell sexy without xy.

Q: What book do women like the most? A: "Their husbands checkbook!"

Q: Did you hear about the woman who couldn't find a singing partner? A: She had to buy a duet yourself kit

Q: What's another meaning for a women? A: Finger puppet

Q: What do girls and noodles have in common? A: They both wiggle when you eat them.

Q: What do you call a letter from a feminist? A: Hate male.

Q: What is the definition of eternity? A: The time that elapses from when you come till she goes.

Q: How do you know your girlfriend is getting fat? A: She fits into your wife's clothes.

Q: Why do men have 2 heads and women 4 lips? A: Cause

men do all the thinking and women do all the talking.

Q: What's the difference between a knife and a woman arguing? A: a knife has a point.

Q: How much money do you need to satisfy a woman? A: It is always just a little bit more.

Q: What have women and condoms got in common? A: If they're not on your dick they're in your wallet.

Q: What do you call a woman who will gives blowjobs for a pair of Jimmy Choos? A: Head Over Heels

Q: How is a woman like an airplane? A: Both have cockpits.

Q: What takes up 12 parking spaces? A: 6 Women drivers.

Q: Why does Beyonce say to the left to the left to the left and not to the right to the right to the right? A: Women don't have rights.

Q: Why do women like to have sex with the lights off? A: They can't stand to see a man have a good time!

Q: What's 6 inches long, 2 inches wide and drives women wild? A: A £100 note.

Q: What do you give a woman with everything? A: Penicillin.

Q: What do you call a woman covered in tattoos? A: Muriel.

Q: How many male chauvinists does it take to change a light bulb? A: None. Let her do the dishes in the dark.

Q: What is woman spelled backwards? A: Kitchen. Female Viagra has been around for years......it's called money!

Q: What's the difference between a woman and a

refrigerator? A: A refrigerator is easier to defrost.

Q: What do toys and women's breasts have in common? A: They were both originally made for kids, but dad ends up playing with

Q: What is love? A: The delusion that one woman differs from another. Monkeys and girls both are same. they fight only for Banana, Boys and rats are same they search only holes.

Q: What do you call a girl with Pms and Esp? A: A bitch who thinks she knows everything.

Q: What's the difference between a woman and a refrigerator? A: A refrigerator doesn't moan when you put meat in it.

Q: What is the difference between your wife and your job? A: After five years your job still sucks.

Q: Why did God create lesbians? A: So feminists couldn't breed.

Q: Why did God give men penises? A: So they'd have at least one way to shut a woman up.

Q: Why do women rub their eyes when they get up in the morning? A: Because they don't have balls.

Q: What do you call a woman who loves small dicks? A: Hopefully your girlfriend.

Q: What do you call a woman that has lost 95% of her intelligence? A: Divorced.

Q: What do you call a sunburnt girl with a yeast infection? A: Grilled cheese

Q: What's easier to pick up the heavier it gets? A: Women.

Q. Why do women talk so much? A. Because they have two sets of lips.

Q: What worse than finding out your wife's got cancer? A: Finding out it's curable.

Q: What's the difference between your bonus and your dick? You don't have to beg a woman to blow your bonus.

Q: Why is a female like a laxative? They both irritate the shit out of you.

Q. What is it when a woman talks dirty to a man? A. £4.99 a minute.

Q: What are the small bumps around a woman's nipples for? A: It's Braille for "suck here".

Q: Did you hear about the guy who finally figured out women? A: He died laughing before he could tell anybody.

Q: Why are hurricanes normally named after women? A: When they come they're wild and wet, but when they go they take your house and car with them.

Q: How many feminists does it take to change a lightbulb? A: None, feminists can't change anything.

Q: What do you call a woman who can't make sandwiches? A: Single.

Q: What do you call a married woman vacuuming? A: Doing what he's told...

Q: Why did God invent the yeast infection? A: So women know what it's like to live with an irritating cunt.

Q: Why don't women blink during foreplay? A: They don't have time.

Q: What's the difference between a girlfriend and wife? A: 45 lbs.

Q: What kind of girlfriend does a potato wants? A: A sweet potato.

Q: What is a vagina? A: The box a penis comes in.

Q: How is a woman like a road? A: Both have manholes.

Q: When do women drink alcohol? A: Wine O'Clock.

Q: Why did God create orgasms? A: So women can moan even when they're happy.

Q: How do you know when it's time to get a new dishwasher? A: When the old one expects you to "do your share"

Q: Why did God make women? A: You think he's gonna wash the dishes?

Q: What's the difference between Jelly and Jam? A: You can't jelly a dick down a woman's throat

Q: What do you call a woman with an opinion? A: Wrong.

Q: What do you call a woman who can't draw? A: Tracy.

Q: What does fucking a woman and cooking an egg in the microwave have in common? A: Both end with a loud, annoying sound and a gooey mess to clean up.

Q: How do you turn a fox into an elephant? A: Marry It!

Q: Why shouldn't you lie to a woman with PMS & GPS? A: Because she's a bitch & she will find you.

Q: Why do women fake orgasms ? A: Because they think men care.

Q: What are the three quickest ways of spreading a rumor (or gossip). A: The internet, Telephone, Tell a woman

Q: What can a lifesaver do for a woman a man can't? A: Cum in five different flavors. How do you make 5 pounds of fat look good? Put a nipple on it.

Q: What's the smartest thing to ever come out a woman's mouth? A: Einstein's cock...

Q: How many men does it take to open a beer? A: None, it should be opened when she brings it to you.

Q: A man runs over his wife. Whose fault is it? A: The man, he shouldn't be driving in the kitchen.

Q: What do you call a hot Indian girl? A: Bomb Bae

Q: Why does a man like to see two women kiss each other? A: Two less mouths that are bitching.

Q: Why can't women drive? A: Because there's no road between the kitchen and the bedroom

Q: What do you call a Chinese woman with an opinion? A: Wong

Q: How can you tell if your wife is dead? A: The sex is the same but the dishes pile up.

Q: Why do Jewish men have to be circumcised? A: Because a Jewish women won't touch anything unless it's 20% off

Q: If your wife keeps coming out of the kitchen to nag at you, what have you done wrong? A: Made her chain too long.

Q: What do you call the new girl at the bank? A: The Nutella!

Q: Why do women wear underwear? A: Because workplace health and safety states 'all manholes must be covered when not in use'!

Q: How is a woman like a condom? A: Both spend more time in your wallet than on your dick.

Q: Why does a bride smile when she walks up the aisle? A: She knows she's given her last blow job.

Q: How do you know when a woman is going to say something intelligent? A: When her first words are,

Why do woman have 3 holes? Because when they get too drunk, you can carry them home like a 6pak!

Boy: "I named my dog after you" Girl: Aww because it's cute.' Boy: "No, because it's a b*tch."

Q: How do you fix a woman's watch? A: You don't, there's a clock on the oven.

Q: What do you call a woman with a frog on her head? A: Lilly.

Q: Why hasn't a female been to the moon ? A: Because it doesn't need cleaning yet!

Q: When is the the only time that a women is right? A: When the kitchen isn't left.

Q: What do you call an all women workplace? A: Unsupervised.

Q: Why do women have smaller feet than men? A: So they can stand closer to the sink.

Q: What's worse than a male chauvinistic pig? A: A woman that won't do what she's told.

Q: Why is a bird another word for a young woman? A: Because women have two cans (toucan).

Q: Why do women wear white on their wedding day? A: So they will match the stove and fridge!

Q: What's the difference between a bitch and a whore? A: A whore fucks everybody at the party, and a bitch fucks everybody at the party EXCEPT YOU.

Q: What's the difference between a Catholic wife and a Jewish wife? A: A Catholic wife has real orgasms and fake jewelry.

Q: Have you heard about the new super-sensitive condoms? A: They hang around after the man leaves and talks to the woman.

Q: Do you know why women fake orgasms? A: Because men fake foreplay.

Q: What's the difference between getting a divorce and getting circumcised? A: When you get a divorce, you get rid of the whole prick!

Q: How is a woman like an airplane? A: Both have cockpits.

Q: What's the difference between a woman and a fridge? A: A fridge doesn't fart when you pull your meat out.

Q: Why can't women read maps? A: Only the male mind can comprehend the concept of one inch equaling a mile.

Q: Why are women like condoms? A: They spend 99% of their time in your wallet, and the other 1% on your dick.

Q: Why did God make man first? A: He didn't want a woman looking over his shoulder.

Q: Why do women have such small feet? A: So they can stand closer to the oven.

Q: How are fat girls and mopeds alike? A: They are fun to ride but you don't want your friends to find out.

Q: Why are there no female astronauts on the moon? A: Because it doesn't need cleaning yet.

Q: What do you call a small parent? A: A minimum!

Q: Why did God give women orgasms? A: So they've got something else to moan about!

Q: Which is the odd one out: a woman, a microwave or a fridge? A: The microwave, the other two leak when they're fucked.

Q: What do you call a girl who doesn't give head? A: You don't!

Q: What's the difference between a woman and a coffin? A: You come in one and go in the other.

Q: What's the difference between PMS and Mad Cow Disease? A: One attacks the cow's brain and sends it fucking mental, the other is an agricultural problem.

Q: How do you know that beer contains female hormones? A: Drink two or three, and you cannot drive properly anymore and start talking bullshit.

Q: What do toy railways and boobs have in common? A: Both are made for children but it's the fathers who play with them most.

Q: Why can't you trust a woman? A: How can you trust something that bleeds for five days and doesn't die?

Q: Why do most men die before their wives? A: They want to!

Q: What food diminishes a woman's sex drive by 90%? A: Wedding Cake!

Q: What do you call a woman who raps about women's rights? A: Feminem

Q: What did the doctor say when a baby was born holding a Starbucks latte? A: "Its a white girl."

Q: What is the difference between a Feminist and a Dog? A: You tell me!

Q: How are women and rocks alike? A: You skip the flat ones!

Q: Why do women stop bleeding when entering menopause? A: Because they need all the blood for their varicose veins.

Q: What is the difference between a cheap hooker and an elephant? A: One rolls on its back for peanuts and the other one lives in a zoo.

Q: What's worse than a male chauvinist pig? A: A woman who won't do as she's told.

Q: Why don't women wear watches? A: There's a clock on the stove.

Q: How to you make a dish washer into a snow blower? A: Give the bitch a shovel

Q: What is the difference between a Woman and a washing machine? A: The washing machine doesn't follow you around for two weeks after you dump a load in it!

Q: How can you tell when a women is having a bad day? A: She has her tampon behind her ear, and she can't find her cigarette.

Q: Why are wives like condoms? A: They both spend too much time in your wallet, and not enough time on the end of your dick.

Q: Why do men die before their wives? A: They want to.

Q: How many men does it take to fix a vacuum cleaner? A: Why the hell should we fix it? We don't use the damn thing.

Q: Why don't they let women play baseball? A: Pitches Be Crazy.

Q: Why do women love orgasms? A: Because it gives them another reason to moan!

Q: What is a woman's favorite rap song? A: Estrogen and juice.

Q: What is a wife? A: An attachment you screw on the bed to get the housework done.

Q: Did you know it's a sin for a woman to make coffee? A: Yup, it's in the Bible. It says . . "He-brews"

Q: How are women like parking spaces? A: The good ones are taken and the rest are handicapped.

Q: Why do women have tits? A: So men will talk to them.

Q: What's the first thing a woman does after coming out of the abuse shelter? A: Cook dinner if she knows what's good for her.

Q: What's the difference between a Woman with PMS and a Pit Bull? A: Lipstick

Q: What do girls and camels have in common? A: They both have camel toes.

Q: What does a woman put behind her ears to make herself more attractive? A: Her ankles.

Q: Why do women close their eyes during sex? A: They can't stand to see a man having a good time.

Q: What did scooby doo say to the lady with the leaky tampon? A: Row row raggy.

Q: Why is our salary like a women's period? A: It comes once in a month ,lasts only for four or five days and if any month it does not come it means your fucked.

Q: What is the definition of "making love"? A: Something a woman does while a guy is fucking her.

Q: Why did God create the orgasm? A: So women can moan even when they're happy.

Q: Who is Eminem's girlfriend? A: The Real Slim Lady.

Q: What's better than winning the WNBA championship? A: Being able to pee standing up.

Q: What is the difference between Feminists and Shit? A: Feminists ain't shit!

Q: How is looking at a Feminist like looking into a Black Void? A: There's nothing there.

Q: What do you call a woman with 4 legs? A: Doggy Style.

Q: What do you call a girl with one leg shorter than the other? A: Eileen

Q: What's the difference between a dog barking in the back yard and a woman yelling on the front porch? A: When you let them in, the dog shuts up.

Q: Why are splinters better than women? A: Splinters are a pain, but they will eventually go away.

Q: Where does a woman with one leg work? A: IHOP.

Q: Why are married women heavier than single women? A: Single women come home, see what's in the fridge and go to bed. Married women come home, see what's in bed and go to the fridge.

I like my women like I like my chicken.
Moist/Tender/Juicy/Fingerlicking Good.

Women are like orange juice cartons, It's not the shape or size or even how sweet the juice is, It's getting those fuckin flaps open

Why did the woman cross the road? Who cares - what was she doing out of the kitchen anyway?

What does the woman who just got out of an abusive relationship do? It better be the damn dishes!

Apparently it was a bad idea to ask Siri "What do women want?" She has been talking nonstop for the last two damn days.

Women on their periods always ovary act.

What is the difference between good girl and a bad girl? The good girl, goes out, goes home and goes to bed. The bad girl, goes out, goes to bed and then goes home.

Women drivers are like stars in the sky. You can see them, but they can't see you

If women are bad at parallel parking, it's only because we've been constantly lied to about what 8 inches is.

Girls are like blackjack, I'm trying to go for 21 but I always hit on 16.

If Lady Gaga is all about being "Born This Way", why does she try so hard to be different?

Women are like blue jeans. They look good for a while but eventually they fade and have to be replaced.

Even if women came with directions, we still wouldn't read them.

The world thinnest book has only one word written in it : EVERYTHING. The book title is : WHAT WOMAN WANT.

Starbucks or Victoria Secrets?.....Who charges more per

cup?

Why do men love their TVs more than their women; They can turn a TV off with just a click.

Every girl is a ninja...It shows when someone touches her phone or her boyfriend.

I met a cute girl buying tampons, so I asked her if I could take her out in 5 to 7 days.

I'm no gynecologist but I know a cunt when I see one.

This woman said she recognized me from vegetarian club, but I'd never met herbivore.

Women fall in love with what they hear, men fall in love with what they can see, that's why women wear makeup and men lie.

Women are like iPhones! You have to touch them all over before they respond.....

Men are like Blackberry! Rub one ball and everything moves!

Achievement seems to be connected with action. Successful men and women keep moving. They make mistakes, but they don't quit.

If men can't focus on two things at once, then why do women have boobs?

If all men are the same, then why does it take a women so long to choose?

The first ten years of a girl's life is spent playing with Barbie's. The next ten years is spent trying to look like one.

Men cheat on good women with bad women. Women choose bad men over good men. The circle of life.

Women fake orgasms to have relationships. Men fake relationships to have orgasms.

Teach a man to fish and can feed a family. Try to teach a woman to fish and she'll be like "You're doing it wrong."

I remember when Barbie was the only girl made of plastic.

All guys should like girls with big thighs. (Why?) Because when they're eating her out, they always have something to keep their cheeks warm.

The biggest difference between men and women is what comes to mind when the word 'Facial' is used.

Why do single women take advice from other single women? That's like Stevie Wonder teaching Ray Charles how to drive.

Women are like cats. They always run away when I try to hold them.

A girl in our gang was called spanner. One look from her would tighten your nuts, her mate was called meteorologist, you could look in her eyes and tell the weather.

I'm looking forward to Alzheimer's, because I'll go to bed with a different woman every night.

Women can bleed for 7 days without dying, Produce milk without eating grass, and bury a bone without digging a hole.

My girlfriend asked me to see things from a woman's point of view...so I looked out the kitchen window.

A gun is just like a woman, it's all about how you hold her.

I asked my wife to let me know next time she has an orgasm but she said that she doesn't like to call me at work.

Women are like wolves. If you want one, you must trap it. Snare it. Tame it. Feed it.

Women who sit on judge's lap, get honorable discharge

Q: What's the difference between a man and a condom? A: Condoms have changed. They're no longer thick and insensitive!

Q: What's the most common sleeping position of a man? A: Around.

Q: What does a penis and an ego have in common? A: All men have one!

Q: What makes a man think about a dinner by candlelight? A: A power failure.

Q: Three words to ruin a man's ego... A: "Is it in?" What is the difference between a man and a vulture? A vulture waits until you're dead before ripping your heart out.

Q: How can you tell if your man is happy? A: Who cares?

Q: How many knees do men really have? A: 3.... right knee, left knee and their wee-knee.

Q: When would you want a man's company? A: When he owns it.

Q: What do you give a man with everything? A: Penicillin.

Q: Why do only 10 percent of men make it to heaven? A: Because if they all went, it would be called hell.

Q: What do you call a Guy who Masturbates more than twice a day? A: A Terrorwrist

Q: What do you call a man with an opinion? A: Wrong.

Q: Why don't women blink during sex? A: There isn't enough time.

Q: What should you give a man who has everything? A: A woman to show him how to work it.

Q: Why do so few men end up in Heaven? A: They never stop to ask directions

Q: How are husbands like lawn mowers? A: They're hard to get started, they emit noxious fumes, and half the time they don't work.

Q: What has eight arms and an IQ of 60? A: Four guys watching a football game.

Q: How can you tell when a man is well hung? A: When you can just barely slip your finger in between his neck and the noose.

Q: How do you get a man to stop biting his nails? A: Make him wear shoes.

Q: How do you find a blind man in a nudist colony? A: It's not hard.

Why are men like lawn mowers? They are difficult to get started, emit foul smells and don't work half the time!

Q: Why doesn't matter how often a married man changes his

job? A: He still ends up with the same boss.

Q. Did you hear about the new "morning after" pill for men? A. It changes their DNA.

Q: What do you call a married man vacuuming? A: Doing what he's told...

Q: Why don't some men have a mid-life crisis? A: They're stuck in adolescence.

Q: Why are Men like parking spaces? A: The good ones are already taken!

Q: Why are men like cars? A: Because they always pull out before they check to see if anyone else is cumming.

Q: How many men does it take to screw in a light bulb? A: One. He just holds it up there and waits for the world to revolve around him.

Q: How many men does it take to screw in a light bulb? A: Three. One to screw in the bulb and two to listen to him brag about the screwing part.

Q: How many men does it take to tile a bathroom? A: Two - if you slice them very thinly.

Q: Why did the man keep going in circles? A: He didn't get the point.

Q: Why can't men get mad cow disease? A: Because they are pigs.

Q: What's the difference between a G-Spot and a golf ball? A: A guy will actually SEARCH for a golf ball.

Q: What do you call a handcuffed man? A: Trustworthy.

Q: What do you call a man with a car on his head? A: Jack

Q: How many men does it take to open a beer? A: none. the lady should already have it open on the table!

Q: What does it mean when a man is in your bed gasping for breath and calling your name? A: You didn't hold the pillow down long enough.

Q: What did the elephant say to the naked man? A: "It's cute but can you pick up peanuts with it?"

Q: How do men define a "50/50" relationship? A: We cook-they eat; we clean-they dirty; we iron-they wrinkle.

Q: What do you call a Roman soldier with a smile on his face and a piece of hair between his two front teeth? A: A GLAD-HE-ATE-HER

Q: How do males exercise on the beach? A: By sucking in their stomachs every time they see a bikini.

Q: What are a married man's two greatest assets? A: A closed mouth and an open wallet.

Q: What is all the fuss about when it comes to men and big boobs? A: They take a lot of lip and they don't talk back.

Q: What do you call 2 guys fighting over a slut? A: Tug-of-whore.

Q: How do you keep your husband from reading your e-mail? A: Rename the mail folder "Instruction Manuals."

Q. Why don't women have men's brains? A. Because they don't have penises to keep them in!

Q: What do bulletproof vests, fire escapes, windshield wipers, and laser printers all have in common? A: All invented by women.

Q: How does a man show he's planning for the future? A: He buys two cases of beer instead of one.

Q: Why do men have 2 heads and women 4 lips? A: Cause men do all the thinking and women do all the talking.

Q: Why did god invent men? A: Because vibrators can't mow the lawn

Q: Why is it difficult to find men who are sensitive, caring and good looking? A: They all already have boyfriends.

Q: How is Colonel Sanders like the typical male? A: All he's concerned with is legs, breasts and thighs.

Q: What did God say after creating man? A: I can do so much better.

Q: What's the difference between men and government bonds? A: Bonds mature.

Q: How do you scare a man? A: Sneak up behind him and start throwing rice!

Q: How is a man like a used car? A: Both are easy to get, cheap, and unreliable!

Q: How do you stop a man from raping you? A: Throw him the remote control.

Q: What do you call a group of men waiting for a haircut? A: A barbercue

Q: What does a man consider a seven-course meal? A: A

pizza and a six pack.

Q: What do you call a man who expects to have sex on the second date? A: Patient!

Q: What is the difference between a man and a tree? A: One is illegal to hit with an ax.

Q: What do you do with a bachelor who thinks he's God's gift to women? A: Exchange him.

Q: What do you call a man who cries while he masturbates? A: A tearjerker.

Q: Why do men whistle when they're sitting on the toilet? A: Because it helps them remember which end they need to wipe.

Q: What do men and mascara have in common? A: They both run at the first sign of emotion.

Q: What do you call a man who never farts in public? A: A private tutor.

Q: What do men and pantyhose have in common? A: They either cling, run, or don't fit right in the crotch!

Q: Why does a penis have a hole in the end? A: So men can be open minded.

Q: What is the difference between a sofa and a man watching Monday Night Football? A: The sofa doesn't keep asking for beer.

Q: What's a man's definition of a romantic evening? A: Sex.

Q: What's the best way to force a male to do sit ups? A: Put the remote control between his toes.

Q: What's the smartest thing a man can say? A: "My wife says..."

Q: How long does it take a man to change the toilet paper? A: We don't know it's never happened.

Q: What's the definition of a woman's perfect lover? A: A man with a nine inch tongue who can breath through his ears.

Q: Why are all dumb blonde jokes one liners? A: So men can understand them.

Q: Why did God create man before woman? A: Because you're always supposed to have a rough draft before creating your masterpiece.

Q: How does a man show he's planning for the future? A: He buys an extra case of beer.

Q: What do you call the useless piece of skin on a penis? A: The man.

Q: Why did God give men penises? A: So they'd have at least one way to shut a woman up.

Q: Why do men have a hole in their penis? A: So their brains can get some oxygen now and then.

Q: Why do men name their penises? A: Because they don't like the idea of having a stranger make 90 percent of their decisions.

Q: Why do men get their great ideas in bed? A: Because their plugged into a genius!

Q: Why do some guys have Red Eyes after Sex? A: Mace.

Q: Why does it take 100 million sperm to fertilize an egg? A: Because not one will stop and ask for directions.

Q: What's a man's idea of honesty in a relationship? A: Telling you his real name.

Q: What's the difference between Big Foot and intelligent man? A: Big Foot has been spotted several times.

Q. How do you drive a man crazy? A. Put a naked woman and a six-pack in front of him. Then tell him to pick only one.

Q: Why did God create man before woman? A: He didn't want any advice.

Q: Why do doctors slap babies' bums right after they're born? A: To knock the penises off the smart ones.

Q: Why did Dorothy get lost on her way to the Emerald City? A: Because she was being led by three boys

Q: What's the difference between a man and E.T.? A: E.T. phones home.

Q: When will a guy ignore even the hottest girl? A: Right after he "comes" inside.

Q: Why do little boys whine? A: Because they're practicing to be men.

Q: What did the elephant say to a naked man? A: Hey that's cute but can you breath through it?

Q. Why do most men prefer cats over dogs? A. Because we hate bitches but we love us some pussy.

For you men who think a woman's place is in the kitchen, remember... that's where the knives are kept.

Every woman should have four pets in her life. A mink in her closet, a jaguar in her garage, a tiger in her bed, and a jackass who pays for everything.

A mother is in the kitchen making dinner for her family when her daughter walks in. "Mother, where do babies come from?" The mother thinks for a few seconds and says, "Well dear, Mommy and Daddy fall in love and get married. One night they go into their bedroom, they kiss and hug, and have sex." The daughter looks puzzled so the mother continues, "That means the daddy puts his penis in the mommy's vagina. That's how you get a baby, honey." The child seems to comprehend. "Oh, I see, but the other night when I came into your room you had daddy's penis in your mouth. What do you get when you do that?" "Jewelry, my dear. Jewelry."

A family is at the dinner table. The son asks the father, "Dad, how many kinds of boobs are there?" The father, surprised, answers, "Well, son, a woman goes through three phases. In her 20s, a woman's breasts are like melons, round and firm. In her 30s and 40s, they are like pears, still nice, hanging a bit. After 50, they are like onions." "Onions?" the son asks. "Yes. You see them and they make you cry." This infuriated his wife and daughter. The daughter asks, "Mom, how many different kinds of willies are there?" The mother smiles and says, "Well, dear, a man goes through three phases also. In his 20s, his willy is like an oak tree, mighty and hard. In his 30s and 40s, it's like a birch, flexible but reliable. After his 50s, it's like a Christmas tree." "A Christmas tree?" the daughter asks. "Yes, dead from the root up and the balls are just for decoration."

A teacher is teaching a class and she sees that Johnny isn't paying attention, so she asks him, "If there are three ducks sitting on a fence, and you shoot one, how many are left?" Johnny says, "None." The teacher asks, "Why?" Johnny says, "Because the shot scared them all off." The teacher says, "No, two, but I like how you're thinking." Johnny asks the teacher, "If you see three women walking out of an ice cream parlor, one is licking her ice cream, one is sucking her ice cream, and one is biting her ice cream, which one is married?" The teacher says, "The one sucking her ice cream." Johnny says, "No, the one with the wedding ring, but I like how you're thinking!"

I asked a Chinese girl for her number. She said, "Sex! Sex! Sex! Free sex tonight!" I said, "Wow!" Then her friend said, "She means 666-3629."

Why did I get divorced? Well, last week was my birthday. My wife didn't wish me a happy birthday. My parents forgot and so did my kids. I went to work and even my colleagues didn't wish me a happy birthday. As I entered my office, my secretary said, "Happy birthday, boss!" I felt so special. She asked me out for lunch. After lunch, she invited me to her apartment. We went there and she said, "Do you mind if I go into the bedroom for a minute?" "Okay," I said. She came out 5 minutes later with a birthday cake, my wife, my parents, my kids, my friends, & my colleagues all yelling, "SURPRISE!!!" while I was waiting on the sofa... naked.

Reporter: "Excuse me, may I interview you?"
Man: "Yes!"
Reporter: "Name?"
Man: "Abdul Al-Rhazim."
Reporter: "Sex?"
Man: "Three to five times a week."
Reporter: "No no! I mean male or female?"
Man: "Yes, male, female... sometimes camel."
Reporter: "Holy cow!"
Man: "Yes, cow, sheep... animals in general."
Reporter: "But isn't that hostile?"
Man: "Yes, horse style, dog style, any style."
Reporter: "Oh dear!"
Man: "No, no deer. Deer run too fast. Hard to catch."

A little girl and boy are fighting about the differences between the sexes, and which one is better. Finally, the boy drops his pants and says, "Here's something I have that you'll never have!" The little girl is pretty upset by this, since it is clearly true, and runs home crying. A while later, she comes running back with a smile on her face. She drops her pants and says, "My mommy says that with one of these, I can have as many of those as I want!"

After picking her son up from school one day, the mother asks him what he did at school. The kid replies, "I had sex with my teacher." She gets so mad that when they get home, she orders him to go straight to his room. When the father returns home that evening, the mother angrily tells him the news of what their son had done. As the father hears the news, a huge grin spreads across his face. He walks to his son's room and asks him what happened at school, the son tells him, "I had sex with my teacher." The father tells the boy that he is so proud of him, and he is going to reward him with the bike he has been asking for. On the way to the store, the dad asks his son if he would like to ride his new bike home. His son responds, "No thanks Dad, my butt still hurts."

A boy says to a girl, "So, sex at my place?" "Yeah!" "Okay, but I sleep in a bunk bed with my younger brother, and he thinks we're making sandwiches, so we have to have a code. Cheese means faster and tomato means harder, okay?" Later on the girl is yelling, "Cheese cheese, tomato tomato!" The younger brother says, "Stop making sandwiches! You're getting mayo all over my bed!"

A man and woman had been married for 30 years, and in those 30 years, they always left the lights off when having sex. He was embarrassed and scared that he couldn't please her, so he always used a big dildo on her. All these years she had no clue. One day, she decided to reach over and flip the light switch on and saw that he was using a dildo. She said "I knew it, asshole, explain the dildo!" He said, "Explain the kids!"

Maria went home happy, telling her mother about how she earned $20 by climbing a tree. Her mom responded, "Maria, they just wanted to see your panties!" Maria replied, "See Mom, I was smart, I took them off!"

Sarah goes to school, and the teacher says, "Today we are going to learn multi-syllable words, class. Does anybody have an example of a multi-syllable word?" Sarah waves her hand, "Me, Miss Rogers, me, me!" Miss Rogers says, "All right, Sarah, what is your multi-syllable word?" Sarah says, "Mas-tur-bate." Miss Rogers smiles and says, "Wow, Sarah, that's a mouthful." Sarah says, "No, Miss Rogers, you're thinking of a blowjob."

A few months after his parents were divorced, little Johnny passed by his mom's bedroom and saw her rubbing her body and moaning, "I need a man, I need a man!" Over the next couple of months, he saw her doing this several times. One day, he came home from school and heard her moaning. When he peeked into her bedroom, he saw a man on top of her. Little Johnny ran into his room, took off his clothes, threw himself on his bed, started stroking himself, and moaning, "Ohh, I need a bike! I need a bike!"

Little Sally came home from school with a smile on her face, and told her mother, "Frankie Brown showed me his weenie today at the playground!" Before the mother could raise a concern, Sally went on to say, "It reminded me of a peanut." Relaxing with a hidden smile, Sally's mom asked, "Really small, was it?" Sally replied, "No, salty." Mom fainted.

A lady goes to the doctor and complains that her husband is losing interest in sex. The doctor gives her a pill, but warns her that it's still experimental. He tells her to slip it into his mashed potatoes at dinner, so that night, she does just that. About a week later, she's back at the doctor, where she says, "Doc, the pill worked great! I put it in the potatoes like you said! It wasn't five minutes later that he jumped up, raked all the food and dishes onto the floor, grabbed me, ripped all my clothes off, and ravaged me right there on the table!" The doctor says, "I'm sorry, we didn't realize the pill was that strong! The foundation will be glad to pay for any damages." "Nah," she says, "that's okay. We're never going back to that restaurant anyway."

A bride tells her husband, "Honey, you know I'm a virgin and I don't know anything about sex. Can you explain it to me first?" "Okay, sweetheart. Putting it simply, we will call your private place 'the prison' and call my private thing 'the prisoner'. So what we do is put the prisoner in the prison." And they made love for the first time and the husband was smiling with satisfaction. Nudging him, his bride giggles, "Honey the prisoner seems to have escaped." Turning on his side, he smiles and says, "Then we will have to re-imprison him." After the second time, the bride says, "Honey, the prisoner is out again!" The husband rises to the occasion and they made love again. The bride again says, "Honey, the prisoner escaped again," to which the husband yelled, "Hey, it's not a life sentence!!!"

At school, Little Johnny's classmate tells him that most adults are hiding at least one dark secret, so it's very easy to blackmail them by saying, "I know the whole truth." Little Johnny decides to go home and try it out.

Johnny's mother greets him at home, and he tells her, "I know the whole truth." His mother quickly hands him $20 and says, "Just don't tell your father." Quite pleased, the boy waits for his father to get home from work, and greets him with, "I know the whole truth." The father promptly hands him $40 and says, "Please don't say a word to your mother."

Very pleased, the boy is on his way to school the next day when he sees the mailman at his front door. The boy greets him by saying, "I know the whole truth." The mailman immediately drops the mail, opens his arms, and says, "Then come give your Daddy a great big hug!"

A man was having premature ejaculation problems so he went to the doctor. The doctor said, "When you feel like you are getting ready to ejaculate, try startling yourself." That same day the man went to the store and bought himself a starter pistol and ran home to his wife. That night the two were having sex and found themselves in the 69 position.

The man felt the urge to ejaculate and fired the starter pistol. The next day he went back to the doctor who asked how it went. The man answered, "Not well. When I fired the pistol, my wife pooped on my face, bit three inches off my penis, and my neighbor came out of the closet with his hands in the air."

One day, there were two boys playing by a stream. One of the young boys saw a bush and went over to it. The other boy couldn't figure out why his friend was at the bush for so long. The other boy went over to the bush and looked. The two boys were looking at a woman bathing naked in the stream. All of a sudden, the second boy took off running. The first boy couldn't understand why he ran away, so he took off after his friend. Finally, he caught up to him and asked why he ran away. The boy said to his friend, "My mom told me if I ever saw a naked lady, I would turn to stone, and I felt something getting hard, so I ran."

There is an overweight guy who is watching TV. A commercial comes on for a guaranteed weight loss of 10 pounds in a week. So the guy, thinking what the hell, signs up for it. Next morning an incredibly beautiful woman is standing at his door in nothing but a pair of running shoes and a sign about her neck that reads, "If you can catch me, you can have me." As soon as he sees her, she takes off running. He tries to catch her, but is unable. This continues for a week, at the end of which, the man has lost 10 pounds. After this he tries the next weight loss plan, 15 pounds in a week. The next morning an even more beautiful woman is standing at the door, in similar conditions. The same happens with her as the first woman, except he almost catches her. This continues for a week, at the end of which he, as suspected, weighs 15 pounds less. Excited about this success, he decides to do the master program. Before he signs up, he is required to sign a waiver and is warned about the intensity of this plan. Still he signs up. The next morning, waiting at the door, is a hulking 300 pound muscle man with nothing but a pair of running shoes, a raging erection, and a sign around his neck that says, "If I catch you, you're mine!" The man was supposed to lose 25 pounds in the week; he lost 34

Q: Which sexual position produces the ugliest children?
A: Ask your mother.

Two cowboys are out on the range talking about their favorite sex position. One says, "I think I enjoy the rodeo position the best." "I don't think I have ever heard of that one," says the other cowboy. "What is it?" "Well, it's where you get your girl down on all four, and you mount her from behind. Then you reach around, cup her t*ts, and whisper in her ear, 'boy these feel almost as nice as your sisters.' Then you try and hold on for 30 seconds."

Kid 1: "Hey, I bet you're still a virgin."
Kid 2: "Yeah, I was a virgin until last night ."
Kid 1: "As if."
Kid 2: "Yeah, just ask your sister."
Kid 1: "I don't have a sister."
Kid 2: "You will in about nine months."

A little boy caught his mom and dad having sex. After, he asked, "What were you and daddy doing?" The mom said, "We were baking a cake." A few days later, the little boy asked his mom, "Were you and daddy baking a cake?" She said yes, and asked him how he knew. He answered, "Because I licked the frosting off the couch."

"Babe is it in?" "Yea." "Does it hurt?" "Uh huh." "Let me put it in slowly." "It still hurts." "Okay, let's try another shoe size."

It was Christmas Eve. A woman came home to her husband after a day of busy shopping. Later on that night when she was getting undressed for bed, he noticed a mark on the inside of her leg. "What is that?" he asked. She said, "I visited the tattoo parlor today. On the inside of one leg I had them tattoo 'Merry Christmas,' and on the inside of the other one they tattooed 'Happy New Year.'" Perplexed, he asked, "Why did you do that?" "Well," she replied, "now you can't complain that there's never anything to eat between Christmas and New Years!"

There is a cucumber, a pickle, and a penis. They are complaining about their lives. The cucumber says, "My life sucks. I'm put in salads, and to top it off, they put ranch on me as well. My life sucks." The pickle says, "That's nothing compared to my life. I'm put in vinegar and stored away. Boy my life boring. I hate life." The penis says, "Why are you

DIRTY, CHEESY AND ABSOLUTELY AWFUL DAD JOKES

guys complaining? My life is so messed up that I feel like shooting myself. They put me in a plastic bag, put me in a cave, and make me do push-ups until I throw up."

A guy walks into a pub and sees a sign hanging over the bar which reads, "Cheese Sandwich: $1.50; Chicken Sandwich: $2.50; Hand Job: $10.00." Checking his wallet for the necessary payment, he walks up to the bar and beckons to one of the three exceptionally attractive blondes serving drinks to an eager-looking group of men. "Yes?" she enquires with a knowing smile, "Can I help you?" "I was wondering," whispers the man, "Are you the one who gives the hand jobs?" "Yes," she purrs, "I am." The man replies, "Well, go wash your hands, I want a cheese sandwich!"

A woman places an ad in the local newspaper. "Looking for a man with three qualifications: won't beat me up, won't run away from me, and is great in bed." Two days later her doorbell rings. "Hi, I'm Tim. I have no arms so I won't beat you, and no legs so I won't run away." "What makes you think you are great in bed?" the woman retorts. Tim replies, "I rang the doorbell, didn't I?"

A typical macho man married a typical good looking lady, and after the wedding, he laid down the following rules. "I'll be home when I want, if I want, what time I want, and I don't expect any hassle from you. I expect a great dinner to be on the table, unless I tell you that I won't be home for dinner. I'll go hunting, fishing, boozing, and card playing when I want with my old buddies, and don't you give me a hard time about it. Those are my rules. Any comments?" His new bride said, "No, that's fine with me. Just understand that there will be sex here at seven o'clock every night, whether you're here or not."

There was an old couple lying in bed. The man turns and tells the woman, "If you want to have sex, pull on my dick once. If you don't want to have sex, pull on my dick one hundred times."

Three guys go to a ski lodge, and there aren't enough rooms, so they have to share a bed. In the middle of the night, the guy on the right wakes up and says, "I had this wild, vivid dream of getting a hand job!" The guy on the left wakes up, and unbelievably, he's had the same dream, too. Then the guy in the middle wakes up and says, "That's funny, I dreamed I was skiing!"

Three brothers are traveling along a road, and their car dies. They all get out of the car, and start walking to a barn that's a little ways away. When they get their, the farmer comes out of the barn, and offers them a room for one night. He says to the first one, "You can sleep with the pigs," the second guy," you can sleep with the cows", and the third guy, "I like the cut of your jib. You can sleep with my 18 daughters." The next morning, he asks everyone how they slept. The first man said, "I slept like a pig." The second man said ,"I slept like a cow." The third guy said, "I slept like a rabbit. I jumped from hole, to hole, to hole."

A trucker who has been out on the road for two months stops at a brothel outside Atlanta. He walks straight up to the Madam, drops down $500 and says, "I want your ugliest woman and a grilled cheese sandwich!" The Madam is astonished. "But sir, for that kind of money you could have one of my prettiest ladies and a three-course meal." The trucker replies, "Listen darlin', I'm not horny – I'm just homesick."

A wife comes home late one night and quietly opens the door to her bedroom. From under the blanket, she sees four legs instead of just her husband's two. She reaches for a baseball bat and starts hitting the blanket as hard as she can. Once she's done, she goes to the kitchen to have a drink. As she enters, she sees her husband there, reading a magazine. He says, "Hi darling, your parents have come to visit us, so I let them stay in our bedroom. Did you say hello?"

The bell rang for school to start and John walked in late. Mr. Clark asked, "John, why are you late?" He replied, "I was on Cherry Hill." Then he sat down. Ten minutes later Nathan walked in late and Mr. Clark repeated, "Why are you late?" Nathan answered, "I was on top of Cherry Hill." Five minutes later Kevin walked in late and Mr. Clark said to him, "Kevin, where have you been?" Kevin replied, "I was on Cherry Hill." Ten minutes later a girl walked in the classroom and Mr. Clark asked, "Hi there, what's your name?" The girl replied,

"Cherry Hill."

Q: Why is sex like math?
A: You add a bed, subtract the clothes, divide the legs, and pray there's no multiplying.

A lawyer married a woman who had previously divorced 10 husbands. On their wedding night, she told her new husband, "Please be gentle, I'm still a virgin." "What?" said the puzzled groom. "How can that be if you've been married 10 times?" "Well, Husband #1 was a sales representative. He kept telling me how great it was going to be. Husband #2 was in software services. He was never really sure how it was supposed to function, but he said he'd look into it and get back to me. Husband #3 was from field services. He said everything checked out diagnostically, but he just couldn't get the system up. Husband #4 was in telemarketing. Even though he knew he had the order, he didn't know when he would be able to deliver. Husband #5 was an engineer. He understood the basic process, but wanted three years to research, implement, and design a new state-of-the-art method. Husband #6 was from finance and administration. He thought he knew how, but he wasn't sure whether it was his job or not. Husband #7 was in marketing. Although he had a nice product, he was never sure how to position it. Husband #8 was a psychologist. All he ever did was talk about it. Husband #9 was a gynecologist. All he did was look at it. Husband #10 was a stamp collector. All he ever did was... God! I miss him! But now that I've married you, I'm really excited!" "Good," said the new husband, "but, why?" "You're a lawyer. This time I know I'm going to get screwed!"

A man gets on a bus, and ends up sitting next to a very attractive nun. Enamored with her, he asks if he can have sex with her. Naturally, she says no, and gets off the bus. The man goes to the bus driver and asks him if he knows of a way for him to have sex with the nun. "Well," says the bus driver, "every night at 8 o'clock, she goes to the cemetery to pray. If you dress up as God, I'm sure you could convince her to have sex with you." The man decides to try it, and dresses up in his best God costume. At eight, he sees the nun and appears before her. "Oh, God!" she exclaims. "Take me with you!" The man tells the nun that she must first have sex with him to prove her loyalty. The nun says yes, but tells him she prefers anal sex. Before you know it, they're getting down to it, having nasty, grunty, loud sex. After it's over, the man pulls off his God disguise. "Ha, ha!" he says, "I'm the man from the bus!" "Ha, ha!" says the nun, removing her costume, "I'm the bus driver!"

I was sitting on my own in a restaurant, when I saw a beautiful woman at another table. I sent her a bottle of the most expensive wine on the menu. She sent me a note, "I will not touch a drop of this wine unless you can assure me that you have seven inches in your pocket." I wrote back, "Give me the wine. As gorgeous as you are, I'm not cutting off three inches for anyone."

A girl realized that she had grown hair between her legs. She got worried and asked her mom about that hair. Her mom calmly said, "That part where the hair has grown is called your monkey. Be proud that your monkey has grown hair." The girl smiled. At dinner, she told her sister, "My monkey has grown hair." Her sister smiled and said, "That's nothing; mine is already eating bananas."

A woman is having a hard time getting her tomatoes to ripen so she goes to her neighbor with her problem. The neighbor says, "All you have to do is go out at midnight and dance around in the garden naked for a few minutes, and the tomatoes will become so embarrassed, they will blush bright red." The woman goes out at midnight and dances around her garden naked for a few minutes. The next morning, the neighbor comes over to the woman's house and asks the woman if her tomatoes have turned red. The woman says "No, they're still green, but I noticed the cucumbers grew four inches!"

An old couple is ready to go to sleep. The old man lies on the bed but the old woman lies down on the floor. The old man asks, "Why are you going to sleep on the floor?" The old woman says, "Because I want to feel something hard for a change."

A gynecologist notices that a new patient is nervous. While putting on the latex gloves, he asks her if she knows how they make latex gloves. The patient says no. The doctor says, "There is a plant in Mexico full of latex that people of various hand sizes dip their hands into and let them dry. She does not crack a smile, but later she laughs. The doctor says, "What's so funny?" She says, "I'm imagining how they make condoms."

There is a fellow who is talking to his buddy and says, "I don't know what to get my wife for her birthday. She has everything, and besides, she can afford to buy anything she wants. I'm stumped." His buddy says, "I have an idea. Why don't you make up a certificate that says she can have two hours of great sex, any way she wants it. She'll probably be thrilled!" The first fellow does just that. The next day, his buddy asks, "Well, did you take my suggestion? How did it turn out?" "She loved it. She jumped up, thanked me, kissed me on the mouth, and ran out the door yelling, 'I'll see you in two hours!'"

During a discussion at Sunday school, a nun asks the children what they think God takes you by when you die. A kid responds, "I think God takes you by your feet, because once I walked into my parents room and my mom's feet were in the air and she was screaming, "Oh God, I'm coming!!!"

What did the left p*ssy lip say to the right p*ssy lip? "We used to be really tight until you let that d*ck come between us."

A guy and his date are parked out in the country away from town, when they start kissing and fondling each other. Just then, the girl stops and sits up. "What's the matter?" asks the guy. She replies, "I really should have mentioned this earlier, but I'm actually a prostitute, and I charge $100 for sex." The man thinks about it for a few seconds, but then reluctantly gets out a $100 bill, pays her, and they have sex. After a cigarette, he just sits in the driver's seat looking out the window. "Why aren't we going anywhere?" asks the girl. "Well, I should have mentioned this before," replies the man, "but I'm actually a taxi driver, and the fare back to town is $50.

A married man was having an affair with his secretary. One day, their passions overcame them in the office and they took off for her house. Exhausted from the afternoon's activities, they fell asleep and awoke at around 8 p.m. As the man threw on his clothes, he told the woman to take his shoes outside and rub them through the grass and dirt. Confused, she nonetheless complied and he slipped into his shoes and drove home. "Where have you been?" demanded his wife when he entered the house. "Darling," replied the man, "I can't lie to you. I've been having an affair with my secretary. I fell asleep in her bed and didn't wake up until eight o'clock." The wife glanced down at his shoes and said, "You liar! You've been playing golf!"

"Daddy, where did I come from?" seven-year-old Rachel asks. It is a moment for which her parents have carefully prepared. They take her into the living room, get out several other books, and explain all they think she should know about sexual attraction, affection, love, and reproduction. Then they both sit back and smile contentedly. "Does that answer your question?" the mom asks. "Not really," the little girl says. "Judy said she came from Detroit. I want to know where I came from."

A man boards a plane with six kids. After they get settled in their seats, a woman sitting across the aisle leans over to him and asks, "Are all of those kids yours?" He replies, "No. I work for a condom company. These are customer complaints."

On hearing that her elderly grandfather has just passed away, Katie goes straight to her grandparents' house to visit her 95-year-old grandmother and comfort her. When she asks how her grandfather has died, her grandmother replies, "He had a heart attack while we were making love on Sunday morning." Horrified, Katie tells her grandmother that two people nearly 100 years old having sex will surely be asking for trouble. "Oh no, my dear. Many years ago, realizing our advanced age, we figured out the best time to do it was when the church bells would start to ring. It was just the right rhythm. It was nice, slow, and even. Nothing too strenuous, simply in on the ding and out on the dong." She pauses, wipes away a tear and then continues, "And if that damned ice cream truck hadn't come along, he'd still be alive today!"

A man joins a soccer team and his new teammates inform him, "At your first team dinner as the new guy, you will have to give us a talk about sex." The evening arrives and he gives a detailed, humorous account of his sex life. When he got home, his wife asked how the evening went and not wanting to lie, but also not wanting to explain exactly what happened, he said, "Oh, I had to make a talk about yachting," his wife thought this a little peculiar but said nothing more and went to sleep. The next day she bumped into one of his new teammates at the supermarket and asked, "I heard my husband had to make a speech last night. How did it go?" His mate said smiling, 'Oh, it was excellent! Your husband is clearly very experienced!." The wife looked confused and replied to his mate, "Strange, he has only done it twice and the second time he was sick."

Scientists have proven that there are two things in the air that have been known to cause women to get pregnant: their legs.

Maria, a devout Catholic, got married and had 15 children. After her first husband died, she remarried and had 15 more children. A few weeks after her second husband died, Maria also passed away. At Maria's funeral, the priest looked skyward and said, "At last, they're finally together." Her sister sitting in the front row said, "Excuse me, Father, but do you mean she and her first husband, or she and her second husband?" The priest replied, "I mean her legs."

Q: What is the difference between Tiger Woods and Santa Claus?
A: Santa stops after three hos.

Three people get arrested and are taken into holding for questioning. The officer talks to the first girl, asking, "What's your name?" She says, "Yo." The officer asks, "What are you in for?" She responds with, "Blowing bubbles." The officer takes her picture and lets her go. He asks the second girl, "What's your name?" She responds with, "Yo Yo." The officer asks, "What are you in for?" She responds with, "Blowing bubbles." The officer takes her picture and lets her go. He talks to the guy and says, "Let me guess, your name is Yo Yo Yo." The guy replies with, "No, it's Bubbles."

A guy decides to do something nice for his girlfriend before they leave on vacation so he gets her name tattooed on his penis. He comes home and shows it to her. She looks at it and says, "That's great, sweetie, but what is 'Wy'?" He tells her to rub it and as she does she sees it actually reads "Wendy." When they arrive at Montego Bay, the couple are walking along a nude beach and the boyfriend notices a black guy with "Wy" on his penis. He asks the man if he also has a girlfriend named Wendy. The black guy laughs and says, "Nah, mon, mine says 'Welcome to Jamaica have a nice day.'"

A little boy with diarrhea tells his mom that he needs Viagra. The mom asks, "Why on Earth do you need that?!" The little boy says, "Isn't that what you give daddy when his sh*t doesn't get hard?"

A guy goes to the store to buy condoms. "Do you want a bag?" the cashier asks. "No," the guy says, "she's not that ugly."

Mickey Mouse is in the middle of a nasty divorce from Minnie Mouse. Mickey spoke to the judge about the separation. "I'm sorry Mickey, but I can't legally separate you two on the grounds that Minnie is mentally insane," said the judge. Mickey replied, "I didn't say she was mentally insane, I said that she's f*cking Goofy!"

A wealthy man was having an affair with an Italian woman for a few years. One night, during one of their rendezvous, she confided in him that she was pregnant. Not wanting to ruin his reputation or his marriage, he paid her a large sum of money if she would go to Italy to have the child. If she stayed in Italy, he would also provide child support until the child turned 18. She agreed, but wondered how he would know when the baby was born. To keep it discrete, he told her to mail him a postcard, and write "Spaghetti" on the back. He would then arrange for child support. One day, about 9 months later, he came home to his confused wife. "Honey," she said, "you received a very strange postcard today." "Oh, just give it to me and I'll explain it later," he said. The wife handed the card over and watched as her husband read the card, turned white, and fainted. On the card was written "Spaghetti, Spaghetti, Spaghetti. Two with meatballs, one without."

A guy and his wife are sitting and watching a boxing match on television. The husband sighs and complains, "This is disappointing. It only lasted for 30 seconds!" "Good," replied his wife. "Now you know how I always feel."

A man is lying on the beach, wearing nothing but a cap over his crotch. A woman passing by remarks, "If you were any sort of a gentleman, you would lift your hat to a lady." He replies, "If you were any sort of a sexy lady, the hat would lift by itself."

Grandma and Grandpa were visiting their kids overnight . When Grandpa found a bottle of Viagra in his son's medicine cabinet, he asked about using one of the pills. The son said, "I don't think you should take one Dad, they're very strong and very expensive." "How much?" asked Grandpa. "$10.00 a pill," answered the son. "I don't care," said Grandpa, "I'd still like to try one, and before we leave in the morning, I'll put the money under the pillow. " Later the next morning, the son found $110 under the pillow. He called Grandpa and said, "I told you each pill was $10, not $110. "I know," said Grandpa. "The hundred is from Grandma!"

They say that during sex you burn off as many calories as running 8 miles. Who the hell runs 8 miles in 30 seconds?

One weekend, a husband is in the bathroom shaving when the local kid Bubba he hired to mow his lawn, comes in to pee. The husband slyly looks over and is shocked at how immensely endowed Bubba is. He can't help himself, and asks Bubba what his secret is. "Well," says Bubba, "every night before I climb into bed with a girl, I whack my penis on the bedpost three times. It works, and it sure impresses the girls!" The husband was excited at this easy suggestion and decided to try it that very night. So before climbing into bed with his wife, he took out his penis and whacked it three times on the bedpost. His wife, half-asleep, said, "Bubba? Is that you?"

Q: What kind of bees make milk instead of honey?
A: Boo-bees

A little boy was in the bath with his mom. The boy said, "What's that hairy thing, mommy?" She replied, "That is my sponge." "Oh yes," said the boy, "The babysitter has got one too. I've seen her washing dad's face with it."

Three words to ruin a man's ego. "Is it in?"

A guy and girl had sex poem competition.
Guy: "Two times two is four, four plus five is nine. I can put mine in yours, but you can't put yours in mine."
Girl: "Two times two is four, four plus five is nine. I know the length of yours, but you won't know the depth of mine."

A man is walking down the street, when he notices that his grandfather is sitting on the porch in a rocking chair, with nothing on from the waist down. "Grandpa, what are you doing?" the man exclaims. The old man looks off in the distance and does not answer his grandson. "Grandpa, what are you doing sitting out here with nothing on below the waist?" he asks again. The old man slyly looks at him and says, "Well, last week I sat out here with no shirt on, and I got a stiff neck. This was your Grandma's idea!"

Mother: "Sweetie, make a Christmas wish."
Girl: "I wish that Santa will send some clothes to those naked girls in papa's computer."

Q: What does the receptionist at the sperm clinic say when clients are leaving?
A: "Thanks for coming!"

Why do women wear panties with flowers on them? In loving memory of all the faces that have been buried there.

A mom of an eight year old boy is awaiting her son's arrival from school. As he runs in, he says he needs to talk to her about making babies. He claims he knows about the development of a fetus, but doesn't understand the answer to the million dollar question. Namely, how does the sperm get into the woman? The mom asks the boy what he thinks the answer is. The boy says that the sperm is manufactured in the man's stomach, rises up to his chest, then throat, and into his mouth, where he then kisses the woman and deposits the sperm into her mouth. The mom tells her boy that it is a good guess, but it's wrong. She gives him a hint by telling him that the sperm comes out of the man's penis. Suddenly, the boy's face becomes quite red and he says, "You mean you put your mouth on that thing?"

A man in a hotel lobby turns to go to the front desk, but he accidentally runs into a woman beside him and his elbow bumps into her breast. They are both quite startled. The man turns to her and says, "Ma'am, if your heart is soft as your breast, I know you'll forgive me." She replies, "If your penis is as hard as your elbow, I'm in room 436."

A boy walks in on his mom and dad having sex. He asks, "What are you doing?" The dad replies, "Making you a brother or sister!" The boy says, "Well, do her doggy style I want a puppy."

A man and his wife go to their honeymoon hotel for their 25th anniversary. As the couple reflected on that magical evening 25 years ago, the wife asked the husband, "When you first saw my naked body in front of you, what was going through your mind?" The husband replied, "All I wanted to do was to f*ck your brains out, and suck your t*ts dry." Then, as the wife undressed, she asked, "What are you thinking now?" He replied, "It looks as if I did a pretty good job."

One day Little Johnny asks his Mum, "How come when I come in to your room you and you're on top of Daddy, you say you're making a sandwich, but after a while I come in again, you're eating a sausage?!"

There was an elderly man who wanted to make his younger

wife pregnant. He went to the doctor to get a sperm count. The doctor told him to take a specimen cup home, fill it, and bring it back. The elderly man came back the next day; the specimen cup was empty and the lid was on it. The doctor asked, "What was the problem?" The elderly man said, "Well, I tried with my right hand... nothing. I tried with my left hand... nothing. So my wife tried with her right hand... nothing. Her left hand... nothing. Her mouth... nothing. Then my wife's friend tried. Right hand, left hand, mouth... still nothing. The doctor replied, "Wait a minute, did you say your wife's friend too?!" The elderly man answered, "Yeah, and we still couldn't get the lid off of the specimen cup."

A newlywed man is going away on a business trip for 3 weeks and doesn't want his brand new bride to get lonely and mess around while he's gone. He stops by the local sex toy shop in town. He looks around, but doesn't see anything that would keep his wife occupied for 3 weeks. He asks the clerk for a recommendation. The clerk takes a black box from underneath the counter, assuring the newlywed that its contents are not for sale. He opens the box, and inside is what appears to be a normal dildo. The newlywed guy is unimpressed, but the clerk says, "Let me demonstrate." He looks at the dildo and says, "Voodoo dick, the counter!" and the dildo jumps out of the box. The clerk commands, "Voodoo dick, the box!" and the dildo hops back into the box. The newlywed man asks how much it costs, but the clerk insists it is a priceless heirloom. The newlywed man takes $500 cash out of his wallet and the clerk quickly hands over the dildo. When the man arrives home, he gives his wife the box, explains how it works, and leaves the next morning on his business trip. A few days later the wife is bored and horny, so she opens the box and skeptically says, "Voodoo dick, my pussy." After about 15 minutes, she has had several orgasms and is starting to get tired, so she tries to pull the voodoo dick out. Her husband had forgotten to tell her how to make it stop. She puts on a dress and drives to the hospital. On the way there, the voodoo dick is still going at her so the lady is speeding and swerving her car. A police officer pulls her over. The cop asks, "Lady, why are you driving so recklessly?" She explains, "Officer, there's this voodoo dick going at my pussy and I can't make it stop! I'm on the way to the hospital to have it removed!" The officer laughs and says, "Yeah right, lady. Voodoo dick, my ass."

An old man goes to a church, and is making a confession:
Man: "Father, I am 75 years old. I have been married for 50 years. All these years I had been faithful to my wife, but yesterday I was intimate with an 18 year old."
Father: "When was the last time you made a confession?"
Man: "I never have, I am Jewish."
Father: "Then why are telling me all this?"
Man: "I'm telling everybody!"

Q: Why is Santa Claus' sack so big? A: He only comes once a year.

A little boy with diarrhea tells his mom that he needs Viagra. The mom asks, "Why on Earth do you need that?!" The little boy says, "Isn't that what you give daddy when his sh*t doesn't get hard?"

A guy goes to the store to buy condoms. "Do you want a bag?" the cashier asks. "No," the guy says, "she's not that ugly."

Mickey Mouse is in the middle of a nasty divorce from Minnie Mouse. Mickey spoke to the judge about the separation. "I'm sorry Mickey, but I can't legally separate you two on the grounds that Minnie is mentally insane," said the judge. Mickey replied, "I didn't say she was mentally insane, I said that she's f*cking Goofy!"

A wealthy man was having an affair with an Italian woman for a few years. One night, during one of their rendezvous, she confided in him that she was pregnant. Not wanting to ruin his reputation or his marriage, he paid her a large sum of money if she would go to Italy to have the child. If she stayed in Italy, he would also provide child support until the child turned 18. She agreed, but wondered how he would know when the baby was born. To keep it discrete, he told her to mail him a postcard, and write "Spaghetti" on the back. He would then arrange for child support. One day, about 9 months later, he came home to his confused wife. "Honey," she said, "you received a very strange postcard today." "Oh, just give it to me and I'll explain it later," he said. The wife handed the card over and watched as her husband read the card, turned white, and fainted. On the card was written "Spaghetti, Spaghetti, Spaghetti. Two with meatballs, one without."

A guy and his wife are sitting and watching a boxing match on television. The husband sighs and complains, "This is disappointing. It only lasted for 30 seconds!" "Good," replied his wife. "Now you know how I always feel."

A man is lying on the beach, wearing nothing but a cap over his crotch. A woman passing by remarks, "If you were any sort of a gentleman, you would lift your hat to a lady." He replies, "If you were any sort of a sexy lady, the hat would lift by itself."

Grandma and Grandpa were visiting their kids overnight . When Grandpa found a bottle of Viagra in his son's medicine cabinet, he asked about using one of the pills. The son said, "I don't think you should take one Dad, they're very strong and very expensive." "How much?" asked Grandpa. "$10.00 a pill," answered the son. "I don't care," said Grandpa, "I'd still like to try one, and before we leave in the morning, I'll put the money under the pillow. " Later the next morning, the son found $110 under the pillow. He called Grandpa and said, "I told you each pill was $10, not $110. "I know," said Grandpa. "The hundred is from Grandma!"

They say that during sex you burn off as many calories as running 8 miles. Who the hell runs 8 miles in 30 seconds?

Why did the bald man cut a hole in his pocket? He wanted to run his fingers through his hair.

There is more money being spent on breast implants and Viagra today, than on Alzheimer's research. This means that by 2040, there should be a large elderly population with perky boobs, huge erections, and absolutely no recollection of what to do with them.

A kid walks up to his mom and asks, "Mom, can I go bungee jumping?" The mom says "No, you were born from broken rubber and I don't want you to go out the same way!"

Q: What did one saggy boob say to the other saggy boob?
A: "We better get some support before someone thinks we're nuts!"

As an airplane is about to crash, a female passenger jumps up frantically and announces, "If I'm going to die, I want to die feeling like a woman." She removes all her clothing and asks, "Is there someone on this plane who is man enough to make me feel like a woman?" A man stands up, removes his shirt and says, "Here, iron this!".

Q: Is Google male or female?
A: Female, because it doesn't let you finish a sentence before making a suggestion.

A young woman was taking golf lessons and had just started

playing her first round of golf when she suffered a bee sting. Her pain was so intense that she decided to return to the clubhouse for medical assistance. The golf pro saw her heading back and said, "You are back early, what's wrong?" "I was stung by a bee!" she said. "Where?" he asked. "Between the first and second hole." she replied. He nodded and said, "Your stance is far too wide."

A man asks, "God, why did you make woman so beautiful?" God responded, "So you would love her." The man asks, "But God, why did you make her so dumb?" God replied, "So she would love you."

How did the medical community come up with the term "PMS"? "Mad Cow Disease" was already taken.

A tough looking group of hairy bikers are riding when they see a girl about to jump off a bridge, so they stop. The leader, a big burly man, gets off his bike and says, "What are you doing?" "I'm going to commit suicide," she says. While he doesn't want to appear insensitive, he also doesn't want to miss an opportunity, so he asks, "Well, before you jump, why don't you give me a kiss?" She does, and it is a long, deep, lingering kiss. After she's finished, the tough, hairy biker says, "Wow! That was the best kiss I've ever had! That's a real talent you're wasting. You could be famous. Why are you committing suicide?" "My parents don't like me dressing up like a girl..."

For all the guys who think a woman's place is in the kitchen, remember that's where the knives are kept.

Girl: "Girls are better than boys."
Boy: "Then why did God make boys first?"
Girl: "Duh, you have to have a rough draft before the final copy."

A boy asks his dad, "What's the difference between potential and realistic?" The dad tells him to go ask the rest of his family if they'd sleep with Brad Pitt for a million dollars, and then he'd tell him the answer. The boy goes up to his mom and asks her. She responds, "A million dollars is a lot of money sweetheart. I could send you, your sister, and your brother to great colleges, so sure, I would!" He then goes and asks his sister to which she replies, "Brad Pitt? Hell ya, he's the hottest guy ever!" Next, the boy asks his brother who replies, "A million dollars? Hell yes I would. I'd be rich!" When the boy excitedly returns to his dad with the family's responses, the dad says, "Well son, potentially, we have three million dollars. Realistically, we have two sluts and a queer."

A man is being arrested by a female police officer, who informs him, "Anything you say can and will be held against you." The man replies, "Boobs!"

There's a new drug for lesbians on the market to cure depression, it's called Trycoxagain.

A man is lying on the beach, wearing nothing but a cap over his crotch. A woman passing by remarks, "If you were any sort of a gentleman, you would lift your hat to a lady." He replies, "If you were any sort of a sexy lady, the hat would lift by itself."

How do you know when a woman is about to say something smart? When she starts her sentence with, "A man once told me..."

A man is drinking in a bar when he notices a beautiful young lady. "Hello there and what is your name?" "Hello," giggles the woman, "I'm Stacey. What's yours?" "I'm Jim." "Jim, do you want to come over to my house tonight?" "Sure!" replies Jim. "Let's go!" At Stacey's house, Jim notices a picture of a man on Stacey's desk and asks, "Is this your brother?" "No, it isn't, Jim!" Stacey giggles. "Is it your husband?" Stacey giggles even more, "No, silly!" "Then, it must be your boyfriend!" Stacey giggles even more while nibbling on Jim's ear. She says, "No, silly!" "Then, who is it?" Stacey replies, "That's me before my operation!"

A man is sitting at a bar enjoying a cocktail when an exceptionally gorgeous, sexy, young woman enters. The man can't stop staring at her. The young woman notices this and walks directly toward him. Before he could offer his apologies for being so rude, the young woman says to him, "I'll do anything you want me to do, no matter how kinky, for

$100, with one condition." Flabbergasted, the man asks what the condition is. The young woman replies, "You have to tell me what you want me to do in just three words." The man considers her proposition for a moment, withdraws his wallet from his pocket, and hands the woman five $20 bills. He looks deeply into her eyes and slowly says, "Paint my house."

How are women and tornadoes alike? They both moan like hell when they come, and take the house when they leave.

An investigative journalist went to Afghanistan to study the culture and was shocked to discover that women were made to walk ten paces behind the men. She asked her guide why and he said, "Because they are considered of lesser status." Outraged the journalist went home. A year later she returned covering violence in the region and was surprised to see the women walking ten paces ahead. She turned to her guide and this time asked, "What has changed?" The guide answered, "Land mines."

Everyone says the world would be better off if it was run by women. Sure, maybe there wouldn't be violence and territorial conquests fueled by male testosterone. But instead, we'd have a bunch of jealous countries that aren't talking to each other.

Q: When can women make you a millionaire? A: When you're a billionaire.

What's six inches long, two inches wide, and drives women wild? Money.

Three guys and a lady were sitting at the bar talking about their professions. The first guy says, "I'm a YUPPIE. You know, young, urban, and professional." The second guy says, "I'm a DINK. You know, double income, no kids." The third guy says, "I'm a RUB. You know, rich urban biker." They turn to the woman and ask, "So what are you?" The woman replies, "I'm a WIFE. You know - Wash, Iron, F***, Etc."

Scientists have discovered a food that diminishes a woman's sex drive by 90%. It's called a wedding cake.

A man driving a car hits a woman. Whose fault is it? The man's. Why was he driving in the kitchen?

PMS jokes aren't funny. Period.

What is easier to pick up the heavier it gets? Women.

When a man opens the car door for his wife, you can be sure of one thing, either the car is new or the wife is.

Life is like a penis: women make it hard for no reason.

Q: Why does it take 1 million sperm to fertilize one egg?
A: Because like all men, they won't stop to ask directions.

Men have two emotions, hungry and horny. If you see him without an erection, make him a sandwich.

A man saw a lady with big breasts. He asked, "Excuse me, can I bite your breasts for $1000?" She agrees, so they go to a secluded corner. She opens her blouse and the man puts his face in her breasts for 10 minutes." Eventually the lady asks, "Aren't you gonna bite them?" He replies, "No, it's too expensive."

Women are like roads. The more curves they have, the more dangerous they are.

Q: Why do Jewish mothers make great parole officers?
A: They never let anyone finish a sentence!

How do you fix a woman's watch? You don't. There is a clock on the oven.

Why do men die before their wives? They want to.

Officer: "Madam, swimming is prohibited in this lake."
Lady: "Why didn't you tell me when I was removing my clothes?"
Officer: "Well, that's not prohibited."

If women aren't supposed to be in the kitchen, then why do they have milk and eggs inside them?!

An old lady was getting on the bus to go to the pet cemetery with her cat's remains. As she got on the bus, she whispered to the bus driver, "I have a dead p*ssy." The driver pointed to the lady sitting behind him and said, "Sit with my wife, you two have a lot in common."

Q: What has eight arms and an IQ of 60?
A: Four guys drinking Bud Light and watching a football game!

Q: What's the difference between a nun and a woman in a bathtub?
A: One has hope in her soul and one has soap in her hole.

Three ladies were on a bus stop bench. One of the ladies looks at the other and asks her if she is Native American,

She says, "Yes, I'm Arapaho." "Is that so?" says the first, "It just happens that I'm a Navajo." The third lady looks at both of them and says, "I'm a Dallas hoe."

One day three women went for a job interview. The man interviewing them posed all three the same question. What would you do if you found an extra €50 in on your paycheck that you shouldn't have received? The first one said, "I'd give it back as it wasn't mine and I wasn't entitled to it." When he asked the second one she replied, "I'd give it to Charity." When he asked the third one, she was more honest and she said, "I'd keep it for myself and go out for a drink." Which one of the three women got the job? The one with the biggest tits!

Three women were trapped on an island. They needed to get across the water to the mainland. They came across a genie who said, "I will grant you ladies three wishes." The first woman said, "Turn me into a fish" and she swam across the water to the other island. The second woman said, "Give me a boat" and she rowed to the other side. The third woman said, "Turn me into a man" and she walked across the bridge.

Q: Why did cavemen drag their women by the hair?
A: Because they found out by dragging them by their legs that their hole would fill up with mud.

Doris is sitting in a bar and says to her friend that she wants to have plastic surgery to enlarge her breasts. The bartender tells her, "Hey, you don't need surgery to do that. I know how to do it without surgery." Doris asks, "How do I do it without surgery?" "Just rub toilet paper between them." Fascinated, Doris says, "How does that make them bigger?" "I don't know, but it sure worked for your ass!"

The average woman would rather have beauty than brains, because the average man can see better than he can think.

How many men does it take to change a roll of toilet paper? I don't know, it has never happened.

Why does it take one million sperm to fertilize one egg? They don't stop and ask for directions.

Jane: "Where are all the kind, considerate, loving men who can show their feelings?"
Jill: "They already have boyfriends.

How does a man show that he is planning for the future? He buys two cases of beer.

What do women and screen doors have in common? The more you bang them, the looser they get.

A boy asked his dad, "What's the difference between a woman and a slave?" His father replies, "I don't know, what?" His son says, "No, I was asking a question."

As an airplane is about to crash, a female passenger jumps up frantically and announces, "If I'm going to die, I want to die feeling like a woman." She removes all her clothing and asks, "Is there someone on this plane who is man enough to make me feel like a woman?" A man stands up, removes his shirt and says, "Here, iron this!"

I have received hundreds of replies to my ad for a husband. They all say the same thing - "Take mine."

There are some girls that like to do something called "homie hopping" and homie hopping is basically a girl dates a guy and then she ends up trying to get with his friends, and then she gets with someone new, then jumps to his other friends, and so on. Guys have this and it's called "testing the waters".

I have discovered the answer to a question that has been puzzling scientists for hundreds of years. What is the exact difference between a split second and a nanosecond? My girlfriend and I were getting ready to go to a movie when, right as we were about to leave home, my girlfriend asked me the question all guys dread. She asked, "Does this make my butt look big?" If I had said "no" in a nanosecond, we'd have been out the door. Since I took a split second, she had to go to the mall and buy new outfits with jewelry, shoes, and purses to match.

What is the mating call of a blond? I'm so drunk. What is the mating call of a brunette? Is that blonde gone yet? What is ther mating call of a redhead? NEXT!

What happens when you give a politician Viagra? He gets taller.

Q: What's the difference between a wife and a mistress?
A: About fifty pounds.

Q: Why is a woman with no breasts a pirate's delight?
A: Because she has a sunken chest.

Little Johnny's teacher gives the class a homework assignment, "Explain the difference between a theory and reality." Little Johnny goes home and is so stumped he asks his sisters ages 21 and 16 for help, and they can't come up with anything either. He then tries asking his father. The father thinks for a bit and replies, "Go to your older sister and ask her if she would suck a guys dick. Then ask her if she would do it for a million dollars. Then go to your younger sister and ask her the same two questions. Write down their answers and bring it back to me." Johnny says, "Okay," and runs off to find his older sister. He asks her the first question and she responds, "Maybe, if I like him." "Would you do it for a million dollars?" She replies, "Hell yes!" He finds the younger sister and asks her the same questions. Her first reply was "Eeeew, no!" but the second answer was "Yeah, sure." Johnny writes down their answers and takes them back to his father. The father looks over them and replies, "There you go." Johnny asks, "What do you mean?" The father says, "Well in theory we have two million dollars, but in reality we have two cocksuckers."

How do you get a dishwasher to dig a hole? Give the woman a shovel!

Q: Why is the space between a woman's breasts and her hips called a waist?
A: Because you could easily fit another pair of breasts there.

There once was a man named Sweeney.
He spilled some gin on his weenie.
That being uncouth,
He dipped it in vermouth,
And slipped his wife a dry martini.

A man is only as faithful as his options.

Q: What's the most expensive Jewish wine?
A: "I wanna go to Florida!"

Q: What do dog poo and women have in common? A: The older they are, the easier they are to pick up.

What do you call a marathon if all the runners are transvestites? A drag race.

After I have sex, I like my woman like my mailbox. Outside my house!

What's the biggest crime committed by transvestites? Male fraud.

What do you do when your wife is staggering? Shoot her again.

God is a woman. I know this because if God was a man, He would have created the whole population female, and only one man. Then, He would have invited that male to the top of the mountain to look down at all the beautiful females. Then God would have gotten jealous and killed him.

What is the difference between a snow man and snow

women?
Snow balls!!

What is the difference between a snow man and a snow woman?
Snowballs!!

Teacher: "Kids, what does the chicken give you?"
Student: "Meat!"
Teacher: "Very good! Now what does the pig give you?"
Student: "Bacon!"
Teacher: "Great! And what does the fat cow give you?"
Student: "Homework!"

Roses are red.
Your blood is too.
You look like a monkey
And belong in a zoo.
Do not worry,
I'll be there too.
Not in the cage,
But laughing at you.

My friend thinks he is smart. He told me an onion is the only food that makes you cry, so I threw a coconut at his face.

A teacher wanted to teach her students about self-esteem, so she asked anyone who thought they were stupid to stand up. One kid stood up and the teacher was surprised. She didn't think anyone would stand up so she asked him, "Why did you stand up?" He answered, "I didn't want to leave you standing up by yourself."

Whenever your ex says, "You'll never find someone like me," the answer to that is, "That's the point."

Q: Which sexual position produces the ugliest children?
A: Ask your mother.

A man goes to a bar and sees a fat girl dancing on a table. He walks over to her and says, "Wow, nice legs!" She is flattered and replies, "You really think so?" The man says, "Oh definitely! Most tables would have collapsed by now."

Yo momma is so fat she uses a pillow for a tampon.

Don't break anybody's heart; they only have 1. Break their bones; they have 206.

If you ever fart in public, just yell, "Turbo power!" and walk faster.

How to be Insulting in Theaters: If the person sitting in front of you is blocking your view, try adopting an irritating cough, or kicking your feet under their seat. Nasty, wet sneezes down the back of their neck are also effective in persuading them to look elsewhere for a seat.

A kid from Mississippi is on Harvard campus for the first time, he stops a student and asks, "Excuse me, can you tell me where the library is at?" The Harvard student replies "At Harvard, you don't end a sentence with a preposition." The kid said, "Sorry about that. Can you tell me where the library is at, asshole?"

Interviewer: "What's your greatest weakness?"
Candidate: "Honesty."
Interviewer: "I don't think honesty is a weakness."
Candidate: "I don't give a f*ck what you think."

How to be insulting when giving directions: Point with four fingers when they ask.

How to be Insulting at Christmas: Try to find what you were given last year and give it back to the person who gave it to you.

How to be Insulting on Public Transportation: Pretend to be foreign when the conductor asks for your fare and try to give him the wrong denomination of money.

How to be insulting at the library: Find the coziest reading nook and start snoring.

Fun fact: If you cut off all your body hair and laid it end to end you'd be a fucking weirdo.

How to be Insulting in Theaters: Noisy wrappings on sweets can be unwrapped at moments of tension when the rest of the theatre is silent.

How to be Insulting at Christmas: Refuse to give any guests a drink, on the grounds that it's for their own good not to drink and drive. Have plenty of soft drinks to offer them though. Then pour yourself a large Scotch, on the grounds that you aren't going anywhere and don't have to worry.

How to be Insulting in Church: Sing out of tune in all the hymns and try singing half a line behind everyone else.

How to be Insulting in the Street: Walk along as if you have stepped in something unpleasant, by pretending to scrape your feet along the pavement, or rubbing your soles on any available patches of grass. Then look daggers at anyone walking a dog.

How to be Insulting in the Street: Approach a complete stranger as if you are about to welcome them warmly, but instead walk straight past and disappear into a shop.

How to be Insulting in the Street: Wave frantically across the street to people who are trying to ignore you and try to attract as much attention to them as you can.

How to be Insulting in the Street: Find a bus stop with a waste bin attached to it. Hide a small bottle of champagne and a leg of chicken in the bottom. Wait for a queue to form at the bus stop, then go and rummage in the gutter, and finally look in the bin. Find the things you've hidden, and devour them in front of the people waiting for the bus.

How to be Insulting in Banks: Take a tape recorder with you to the meeting with the manager. Say nothing the entire time, but simply record all he says to you. Then when he's finished play it back to him at twice the speed and leave.

How to be Insulting on the Beach: Sit by the water with a fishing rod, and throw revolting lumps of old bread into the water where the children are enjoying themselves.

How to be Insulting in Hotels: If you have to get up early, do it with the maximum amount of noise. Run a bath loudly and sing in it.

How to be Insulting at Christmas: Turn up the television when the carol singers arrive and turn off the lights until they go away.

How to be Insulting to Neighbors: On moving in, erect a fence at least six feet high, with a garish finish on their side.

How to be Insulting Abroad: Ask for local delicacies and leave them on your plate.

How to be Insulting in Hotels: Call room service last thing at night, when the kitchens have just been locked, and ask for a cheese sandwich and a glass of fresh milk. Make sure that you leave them untouched and conspicuous the next morning.

How to be Insulting on the Beach: Try to find seaweed and drag this along the beach, leaving bits beside other people's places.

How to be Insulting in Church: Pour water into the font and wash your hands in it. If you're really daring, take off your shoes and socks and cool your feet.

How to be Insulting in Church: If you just want to look inside the church, go in when you see the sign 'Service in Progress'. Take photographs with a bright flash-gun.

How to be Insulting at Christmas: Buy crackers without any little gifts inside. If you have the time beforehand, put unpleasant little remarks and observations inside them instead. You might try to glue the paper hats together so that they tear when the guests try to open them.

How to be Insulting in Banks: Try to use one of the automatic cash dispensers, but use it incorrectly. If it's inside the bank, do this until someone is sent to help you out, or until you're asked to leave. If it's outside the bank, kick the machine and try to open it with your car keys, a penknife or your umbrella.

How to be Insulting on the Beach: If there's enough sand, dig huge walls around your site and try to put your neighbors in the shade.

How to be Insulting in Church: Arrive late for any service and arrive noisily. Forget at least one, if not both books, and try to make others stand up while you go back for the ones you need.

How to be Insulting at Christmas: Try to duplicate presents

wherever possible then lose the receipts so that none of them can be exchanged. If they happen to be things you want yourself, so much the better. Just offer to take them back.

How to be Insulting in Banks: When ordering travelers checks, try to get the smallest denomination available, and then take ages signing each check in front of the cashier.

How to be Insulting in Church: Always try to be half a line ahead of the vicar, and always be as loud as you dare in the responses.

How to be Insulting in Banks: Put your old sandwiches into the night safe pouch and complain by letter when it's returned to you empty.

How to be Insulting Abroad: Insist on paying for everything in sterling.

Don't be racist; racism is a crime; and crime is for black people.

How do you starve a black person? Put their food stamp card under their workboots!

Q: How does a black girl tell if she is pregnant? A: When she pulls the tampon out all the cotton is picked.

I was at my bank today waiting in a short line. There was just one lady in front of me, an Asian lady, who was trying to exchange yen for dollars. It was obvious she was a little irritated. She asked the teller, "Why it change? Yesterday, I get two hunat dolla of yen. Today I only get hunat eighty? Why it change?" The teller shrugged his shoulders and said, "Fluctuations." The Asian lady says, "Fluc you white people too!"

An old man takes his grandson fishing in a local pond one day. After 20 minutes of fishing, the old man fires up a cigar. The young boy asks, "Grandpa, can I have a cigar?" The old man asks, "Son, can your d*ck touch your asshole?" The young boy says no. "Then u can't have a cigar." Another 20 minutes passes, and the old man opens a beer. The young boy asks, "Grandpa, can I have a beer?" The old man asks, "Son, can your d*ck touch your asshole?" The young boy says no. "Well, then u can't have a beer." Another 20 minutes passes, and the young boy opens a bag of potato chips. The old man asks, "Son, can I have some of your chips?" The boy asks, "Well, Grandpa, can your d*ck touch your asshole?" The old man says, "It sure can." The boy says, "Well good, then go f*ck yourself, these are my chips."

Jill goes home one night with a guy she met at a club. He's tall, super hot, and seems different than most guys she meets. They arrive at his place and head straight to his room. Jill can't help but notice a shelf full of teddy bears. On the bottom are small teddy bears, on the middle are medium-sized teddy bears, and finally, on the top are large teddy bears, all lined up beside each other. She begins to think that he is sentimental and sweet, and isn't afraid to show it. Her heart melts and she want to give him the best night of his life. She gives him a bl*wjob, and lets him really give it to her, and even takes it in the rear! In the morning, she slowly gets dressed, and smiles at him and asks, "How was that?" He nods and says, "Not too f*ckin' bad at all. Help yourself to a prize on the second shelf!"

Helen Keller walks into a bar, then a table, then a chair.

What do you call a cow with no legs? Ground beef.

Q: What did the cannibal do after dumping his girlfriend?
A: He wiped his bum.

A man sitting at a bar asked a pretty woman sitting next to him, Excuse me, but can I smell your pussy?" "Get away from me, you pervert," she replied. "Oh, I'm sorry," exclaims the man, "It must be your feet."

Four gay guys are sitting in a Jacuzzi when all of a sudden, a condom starts floating. One of the gay guys turns around and asks, "Okay, who farted?"

So this dude comes home from work one day, and his wife is watching the Food Network. The husband asks, "Why do you watch that? You still cant cook," and the wife responds, "Why do you watch porn? You still cant f*ck."

What do you say when you see your television floating at night? "Drop it nigga."

In South Los Angeles, a fourplex was destroyed by fire. A Nigerian family of six con artists lived on the first floor, and all six died in the fire. A black Islamic group of seven welfare cheaters, all illegally in the country from Kenya, lived on the second floor, and they, too, all perished in the fire. Six Los Angeles gangbanger ex-cons lived on the third floor and they died as well. One white couple lived on the top floor. The couple survived the fire. Jesse Jackson, John Burris, and Al Sharpton were furious. They flew to Los Angeles and met with the fire chief on television. They loudly demanded to know why the Nigerians, Muslims, and gangbangers all died in the fire, and only the white couple survived. The fire chief said, "Please don't get upset. The reason those fellow citizens survived was because they were at work."

A limbless man sat on the side of a lake everyday. He had no hands or no legs. One day he was crying when a woman was walking by and saw that he was upset, so she asked if he was okay. He replied, "No." The woman said, "Well, what's wrong?" The limbless man said, "I've never been hugged by anyone ever." So the woman, out of kindness, hugged the man. "Are you okay now?" she asked. "No," the man replied. So again the woman asked him what was wrong. He answered, "I've never been kissed before." The woman eagerly gave him a peck on the lips and asked, "Are you okay now?" The man shook his head sadly. The woman asked him what was wrong for the third time. The man said, "I've never been fucked." The woman looked at him, picks him up, throws him in the lake, and says, "Now you are!"

Q. What do you call a nun in a wheelchair?
A. Virgin Mobile.

Q: What do KFC and pussy have in common?
A: Both are finger lickin' good and after you are done eating you have a box to put the bone in.

So there's a black guy, a white guy, and a Mexican. They find a genie's lamp, they rub it, and poof appears the genie! The genie goes to the black guy and asks, "What's your one wish?" The black guy goes, "I wish for me and all my people to be back in Africa, happy and everything." So poof! His wish is granted. Then, the genie goes to the Mexican and asks, "What's your one wish?" The Mexican goes, "I wish for me and all my people to be in Mexico, happy and everything." So poof! His wish is granted. Now, the genie goes over to the white guy and asks, "What's your one wish?" and the white guy asks, "You mean to tell me that all the black and Mexican people are out of America?" The genie replies, "Yes." So the white guy goes, "Then I'll have a Coke."

Michael Jackson has done something no one has ever done before. I'm not talking about his record sales or tickets sold. I'm talking about being born a black man, and dying a white woman. Incredible.

There was this homeless drunk dude laying in an alley talking out loud saying, "I wish had another drink." He then passed out. As he was saying that, a gay dude was walking by and heard him. When the gay guy came back, he f*cked the homeless guy and put three dollars in his pocket. The homeless dude woke up later and found the money, ran to the liquor store, and said, "Give me the cheapest half of pint you have," and went back to his spot, drunk it and passed out again. The gay dude came back, f*cked the homeless dude again, and left five dollars. He ran back to the liquor store and said, "Give me the cheapest pint you have," and went back to his spot. The gay dude came back again. Once he saw the homeless man passed out, he f*cked him again and left eight dollars The homeless dude woke up and realized he had some more money. He ran back to the liquor store, and before he could say a word, the owner said, "I know, you want the cheapest pint you can get," and the homeless dude said, "No, give me the most expensive half you got. That cheap liquor is tearing my ass up."

What is better than winning the gold medal at the Special Olympics? Having arms and legs.

What is the difference between acne and a Catholic priest? Acne usually comes on a boy's face after he turns 12.

What is the difference between Jesus, and a picture of Jesus? You can hang the picture with just one nail.

There is a white boy, a Mexican boy, and a black boy who are all in the fifth grade. Who has the biggest d*ck? The black boy, because he's 18.

A blind man walked into a fish market and said, "Hello ladies!"

There's a man walking a tight rope 60 feet above ground. There's another man getting a bl*wjob from a 60 year old woman. What are they both thinking at the exact same time? Don't look down, don't look down, don't look down, don't look down!

This brother was banging his sister, and he says, "You f*ck like Mom," and she laughs. He says, "What?" She says,

"That's what Dad said."

How come there aren't any Mexicans on Star Trek? They don't work in the future, either.

The difference between like and love is spit and swallow.

Q: Why is a woman with no breasts a pirate's delight?
A: Because she has a sunken chest.

A man recently had his arm amputated and decided to kill himself by jumping off a building. When he was ready to jump, he saw a man with both arms amputated dancing around. He decided to find out why he was so happy. The man told him, "I'm not dancing. My ass is itching and I can't scratch it!"

Here is a pick up line. "Hey girl, come sit on my lap and we could talk about the first thing that pops up."

My girlfriend called me a pedophile; that's a big word for a nine year old

A woman was at the pharmacy and asked, "Can I get Viagra here?" The old pharmacist replied, "Yes." She asked, "Can I get it over the counter?" He responded, "If you give me two of them, you can."

When I was a kid, my father would tell me that the black Santa Claus was coming to our house for Christmas. So, instead of putting out cookies and milk, we would put out cornbread and purple kool-aid.

Three ladies were on a flight, when suddenly the captain announced, "Please prepare for a crash landing." The first lady put on all her jewelry. Surprised by this, the other ladies questioned her actions. The first lady replied, "Well, when they come to rescue us they will see that I am rich, and will rescue me first." The second lady, not wanting to be left behind, began to take off her top and bra. "Why are you doing that?" the other ladies questioned. "Well, when they come to rescue us, they will see my great t*ts and will take me first." The third lady who was African, not wanting to be outdone, took off her pants and panties. "Why are you doing that?" the other ladies questioned. "Well, they always search for the black box first."

Q: What do elephants use for tampons?
A: Sheep.

Have you heard? Michael Jackson's last wish was that his body be turned into Legos. So little kids can play with him. It turns out this wish hasn't been difficult to implement, as his body was already 99% plastic.

Q: What do you call a cheap circumcision?
A: A rip off.

Why is it that skinny men like fat women? Because they need warmth in winter and shade in summer.

Q: How do you turn a cat into a fish?
A: Tell the woman not to wash down there.

Q: What do you do when an epileptic has a seizure in the bath tub?
A: Throw in some laundry.

How do you know if a guy has a high sperm count? She has to chew before she swallows.

After being married for twenty years to his lover, a gay man dies. When the funeral arrangements have been set, the widower approaches the undertaker with a peculiar request, "I know we had plans to cremate his body, but will you please chop him up and put him in a extra spicy curry instead?" The undertaker asks, "Why would you want that?" The gay widower replies, "So he will blow my ass out one more time."

Ever seen a blind man swim? He probably hasn't either.

A child and a child molester walk into a forest together. The child turns to the molester and says, "Boy, these woods are scary." The molester says to the child, "You think you're scared? I have to walk out of here alone."

What's the difference between parsley and pubic hair? Nothing. Push them both over and keep on eating.

The tenderest love is between two homosexual men with hemorrhoids.

The myth about blacks having big penises is true. Asians have small eyes because you have to squint to see their penis.

What's black, white, and red all over? A nun on her period.

Well, I was just thinking about all the possible things that could make the new president comfortable in the White House. Putting graffiti on the walls of the White House that says, "Cheney was here," or changing the president's theme from "Hail to the Chief," to the Jeffersons' show's theme song, "We're moving on up."

Why do women have one more brain cell than a horse? For managing not to drink the water from the bucket while she sweeps the floor.

Q: What kind of wood doesn't float?
A: Natalie Wood.

Q: What's green and eats meat?
A: Syphilis.

What do you call a cholo with one short leg and one regular leg? Not even a!

Q: What do you call a lady that is stuck to a lamppost?
A: A lamppost lady.

Yo momma is so fat, I took a picture of her last Christmas and it's still printing.

Yo momma is so fat when she got on the scale it said, "I need your weight not your phone number."

Yo momma is so fat that when she went to the beach a

whale swam up and sang, "We are family, even though you're fatter than me."

Yo mamma is so ugly when she tried to join an ugly contest they said, "Sorry, no professionals."

Yo momma's so fat and old when God said, "Let there be light," he asked your mother to move out of the way.

Yo momma's so fat, that when she fell, no one was laughing but the ground was cracking up.

Yo momma is so fat when she sat on WalMart, she lowered the prices.

Yo momma is so stupid when an intruder broke into her house, she ran downstairs, dialed 9-1-1 on the microwave, and couldn't find the "CALL" button.

Yo momma is so fat that Dora can't even explore her!

Your momma is so ugly she made One Direction go another direction.

Yo momma is so fat her bellybutton gets home 15 minutes before she does.

Yo momma's so dumb, when y'all were driving to Disneyland, she saw a sign that said "Disneyland left," so she went home.

Yo momma is so stupid she climbed over a glass wall to see what was on the other side.

Yo momma is so hairy, when she went to the movie theater to see Star Wars, everybody screamed and said, "IT'S CHEWBACCA!"

Yo momma so stupid she stuck a battery up her ass and said, "I GOT THE POWER!"

Yo momma is so stupid she brought a spoon to the super bowl.

Yo mamma is so fat she doesn't need the internet, because she's already world wide.

Yo Momma's so fat when I told her to touch her toes she said, "What are those"?

Yo momma is so fat, when she sat on an iPod, she made the iPad!

Yo momma's so fat she needs cheat codes for Wii Fit.

Yo mamma is so ugly when she took a bath the water jumped out.

Yo momma is so fat when she went to KFC the cashier asked, "What size bucket?" and yo momma said, "The one on the roof."

Yo momma is so stupid she took a ruler to bed to see how long she slept.

Yo momma is so fat that when she saw a yellow school bus go by full of white kids she ran after it yelling, "TWINKIE!"

Yo momma's so fat, that when she went to the zoo, the hippos got jealous.

Your momma's so ugly, when she goes into a strip club, they pay her to keep her clothes on.

Yo mama so ugly when she went into a haunted house she came out with a job application.

Yo momma is so ugly even Hello Kitty said, "Goodbye" to her

Yo mamma is so fat she walked past the TV and I missed 3 episodes.

Yo momma so fat when she steps out in a yellow raincoat, the people yell, "TAXI!"

Yo momma is so stupid when your dad sad it was chilly outside, she ran out the door with a spoon!

Yo momma is so poor I saw her kicking a trash can so I asked, "What are you doing?" and she said, "I'm moving."

Yo momma is so fat she sat on the rainbow and Skittles came out.

Yo mom is so dumb that she thought Dunkin' Donuts was a basketball team.

Yo momma's so fat, she got baptized at Sea World.

Yo mamma is so ugly, she scared the shit out of the toilet.

Yo momma's so fat, she has more rolls than a bakery.

Yo momma is so ugly Fix-It Felix said, "I can't fix it."

Yo mama so fat I tried driving around her and I ran out of gas.

Yo momma is so stupid that when thieves broke in and stole the tv, she ran outside and yelled to them, "Hey, you forgot the remote!"

Yo momma is so fat when she stepped on the scale it read, "Get the hell off me!"

Yo momma is so ugly she turned Medusa into stone.

Yo momma is so stupid that she sat on the TV to watch the couch.

Yo momma is so old, I slapped her in the back and her boobs fell off.

Yo momma's so fat, she wore a black bathing suit to the pool and everyone yelled "oil spill!"

Yo momma's so fat, the only way to get her out of a telephone booth is to grease her thighs and throw a Twinkie in the street.

Yo momma is so fat, when she sat on the back of the bus it did a wheelie.

Yo momma's so fat, her baby pictures were taken by satellite.

Yo Momma's teeth are so yellow, that when she smiles, traffic slows down!

Yo momma's so fat she can't even jump to a conclusion.

Yo momma's so ugly, the government moved Halloween to her birthday!

Yo momma is so ashy, every time she rubs her arms it snows.

Yo momma's so fat, she tripped over Wal-Mart, stumbled over K-Mart, and landed on Target.

Yo mama so stupid, she got hit by a parked car.

Yo mama's so stupid she put paper on the television and

called it paper view.

Yo momma is so poor that when I asked her what's for dinner tonight she lit her pocket on fire and said, "hot pocket."

Yo mama's so fat when I pictured her in my head she broke my neck.

Yo momma so ugly, she had to get the baby drunk so that she could breastfeed it.

Your momma is so stupid she put airbags on her computer in case it crashed.

Yo mama so stupid, she returned a donut because it had a hole in it.

Yo mamma so stupid she tried to put M&M's in alphabetical order.

Yo momma's so ugly, her birth certificate is an apology letter from the condom factory.

Yo momma is so short, you can see her feet on her driver's license.

Yo momma's so fat that Mount Everest tried to climb her.

Yo momma's so smelly, that when she spread her legs, I got seasick.

What happens to a frog's car when it breaks down?
It gets toad away.

A boy is selling fish on a corner. To get his customers' attention, he is yelling, "Dam fish for sale! Get your dam fish here!" A pastor hears this and asks, "Why are you calling them 'dam fish.'" The boy responds, "Because I caught these fish at the local dam." The pastor buys a couple fish, takes them home to his wife, and asks her to cook the dam fish. The wife responds surprised, "I didn't know it was acceptable for a preacher to speak that way." He explains to her why they are dam fish. Later at the dinner table, he asks his son to pass the dam fish. He responds, "That's the spirit, Dad! Now pass the f*cking potatoes!"

A blonde and a redhead have a ranch. They have just lost their bull. The women need to buy another, but only have $500. The redhead tells the blonde, "I will go to the market and see if I can find one for under that amount. If I can, I will send you a telegram." She goes to the market and finds one for $499. Having only one dollar left, she goes to the telegraph office and finds out that it costs one dollar per word. She is stumped on how to tell the blonde to bring the truck and trailer. Finally, she tells the telegraph operator to send the word "comfortable." Skeptical, the operator asks, "How will she know to come with the trailer from just that word?" The redhead replies, "She's a blonde so she reads slow: 'Come for ta bull.'"

A teacher asked her students to use the word "beans" in a sentence. "My father grows beans," said one girl. "My mother cooks beans," said a boy. A third student spoke up, "We are all human beans."

Q: Why was six scared of seven?
A: Because seven "ate" nine.

Q: Can a kangaroo jump higher than the Empire State Building?
A: Of course. The Empire State Building can't jump.

Instead of "the John," I call my toilet "the Jim." That way it sounds better when I say I go to the Jim first thing every morning.

Q: What is the difference between snowmen and snowwomen?
A: Snowballs.

Q: Did you hear about the kidnapping at school?
A: It's okay. He woke up.

A lady comes home from her doctor's appointment grinning from ear to ear. Her husband asks, "Why are you so happy?" The wife says, "The doctor told me that for a forty-five year old woman, I have the breasts of a eighteen year old." "Oh yeah?" quipped her husband, "What did he say about your forty-five year old ass?" She said, "Your name never came up in the conversation."

Q: How do you count cows?
A: With a cowculator.

I never wanted to believe that my Dad was stealing from his job as a road worker. But when I got home, all the signs were there.

Q: What starts with E, ends with E, and has only 1 letter in it?
A: Envelope.

Q: Why couldn't the leopard play hide and seek?
A: Because he was always spotted.

Q: How do astronomers organize a party?
A: They planet.

Q: What do you call a bear with no teeth?

A: A gummy bear.

Q: Why does Humpty Dumpty love autumn?
A: Because Humpty Dumpty had a great fall.

A man is being arrested by a female police officer, who informs him, "Anything you say can and will be held against you." The man replies, "Boobs!"

I was wondering why the ball kept getting bigger and bigger, and then it hit me.

Q: Why did the can crusher quit his job?
A: Because it was soda pressing.

A man got hit in the head with a can of Coke, but he was alright because it was a soft drink.

Q: What do computers eat for a snack?
A: Microchips!

Mother superior tells two new nuns that they have to paint their room without getting any paint on their clothes. One nun suggests to the other, "Hey, let's take all our clothes off, fold them up, and lock the door." So they do this, and begin painting their room. Soon they hear a knock at the door. They ask, "Who is it?" "Blind man!" The nuns look at each other and one nun says, "He's blind, so he can't see. What could it hurt?" They let him in. The blind man walks in and says, "Hey, nice tits. Where do you want me to hang the blinds?"

THREE TREES AND A WOODPECKER
Two tall trees, a birch and a beech, are growing in the woods. A small tree begins to grow between them, and the

beech says to the birch, "Is that a son of a beech or a son of a birch?" The birch says he cannot tell, but just then a woodpecker lands on the sapling.

The birch says, "Woodpecker, you are a tree expert. Can you tell if that is a son of a beech or a son of a birch?"

The woodpecker takes a taste of the small tree and replies, "It is neither a son of a beech nor a son of a birch, It is, however, the best piece of ash I have ever poked my pecker into."

Now wipe that smile off your face.

Q: Can February march?
A: No, but April may.

Why is it that your nose runs, but your feet smell?

Q: What did the blanket say when it fell of the bed?
A: "Oh sheet!"

Q: What is the tallest building in the entire world?
A: The library, because it has so many stories.

Q: Why can't you trust an atom?
A: Because they make up everything.

If you ever get cold, just stand in the corner of a room for a while. They're normally around 90 degrees.

Q: What do you call two Mexicans playing basketball?
A: Juan on Juan.

Q: Why did the school kids eat their homework?
A: Because their teacher told them it was a piece of cake.

Whoever invented knock knock jokes should get a no bell prize.

Q: What's the difference between a guitar and a fish?
A: You can tune a guitar, but you can't tuna fish.

Q: What is the difference between a cat and a comma?
A: One has claws at the end of its paws and the other is a pause at the end of a clause.

If the right side of the brain controls the left side of the body, then lefties are the only ones in their right mind

Q: What's the best thing about Switzerland?
A: I don't know, but the flag is a big plus.

Q: Why is England the wettest country?
A: Because so many kings and queens have been reigning there.

Johnny was at school and the teacher said, "Someone use fascinate in a sentence." Sally answered, "The zoo was fascinating." The teacher said, "Sorry, Sally, I said to use fascinate in a sentence." Maria suggested, "I was fascinated at the zoo." Once again the teacher said, "No, Maria, I specifically said to use fascinate in a sentence." Johnny said, "My sister has ten buttons on her sweater." Again the teacher said, "Sorry, Johnny, I said use fascinate in a sentence." Johnny replied, "I know, but her boobs are so big she can only fasten eight."

Q: What did the big chimney say to the little chimney?

A: "You're too young to smoke."

Q: Did your hear about the man with a broken left arm and broken left leg?
A: Don't worry he's "ALRIGHT" now!

PMS jokes aren't funny. Period.

Q: How do trees access the internet?
A: They log in.

On the first day of school, the teacher asked a student, "What are your parents' names?" The student replied, "My father's name is Laughing and my mother's name is Smiling." The teacher said, "Are you kidding?" The student said, "No, Kidding is my brother. I am Joking."

Q: What is Mozart doing right now?
A: Decomposing.

Q: What type of sandals do frogs wear?
A: Open-toad!

A drunk walks into a bar with jumper cables around his neck. The bartender says, "You can stay but don't try to start anything."

Q: What do you call stoned Mexicans?
A: Baked beans.

"Give it to me! Give it to me!" she yelled, "I'm so wet, give it to me now!" She could scream all she wanted to. I was keeping the umbrella.

Q: What is the difference between a teacher and a train?
A: One says, "Spit out your gum," and the other says, "Choo choo choo!"

Two men broke into a drugstore and stole all the Viagra. The police put out an alert to be on the lookout for the two hardened criminals.

Q: What happens once in a minute and twice in a moment but never in a decade?
A: The letter "m."

Q: What's the difference between a cat and a complex sentence?
A: A cat has claws at the end of its paws and a complex sentence has a pause at the end of its clause.

Helium walks into a bar and asks for a drink. The bartender says, "Sorry, we don't serve noble gases here." Helium doesn't react.

Q: Why shouldn't you write with a broken pencil?
A: Because it's pointless!

A man was driving and saw a truck stalled on the side of the highway that had ten penguins standing next to it. The man pulled over and asked the truck driver if he needed any help. The truck driver replied, "If you can take these penguins to the zoo while I wait for AAA that will be great!" The man agreed and the penguins hopped into the back of his car. Two hours later, the trucker was back on the road again and decided to check on the penguins. He showed up at the zoo and they weren't there! He headed back into his truck and started driving around the town, looking for any sign of the penguins, the man, or his car. While driving past a movie theater, the truck driver spotted the guy walking out with the ten penguins. The truck driver yelled, "What are you doing? You were supposed to take them to the zoo!" The man replied, "I did and then I had some extra money so I took them to go see a movie."

Q: What do you get when you cross a fish and an elephant?
A: Swimming trunks.

Q: How come oysters never donate to charity?
A: Because they are shellfish.

Q: What do you call someone without a nose or a body?
A: Nobodynose.

Innkeeper: "The room is $15 a night. It's $5 if you make your own bed."
Guest: "I'll make my own bed."
Innkeeper: "Good. I'll get you some nails and wood."

A little girl and her older brother were visiting their grandfather's farm. The older brother decided to play a trick on his younger sister. He told her that he discovered a man-eating chicken. The girl was frightened, and ran inside in fear. Then the older brother heard his little sister scream. He ran inside immediately. She was screaming at their grandfather, who was chowing down on a plate of fried chicken. "What is it?" he asked. The sister turned to him in fear and said," It- it's- IT'S A MAN EATING CHICKEN!!!"

One night a lady came home from her weekly prayer meeting, found she was being robbed, and she shouted out, "Acts 2:38: 'Repent & be baptized & your sins will be forgiven.'" The robber quickly gave up & the lady rang the police. While handcuffing the criminal, a policeman said, "Gee mate, you gave up pretty easily. How come you gave up so quickly?" The robber said, "She said she had an axe and two 38's!"

Q: Why did the scarecrow get promoted?

A: Because he was outstanding in his field.

Q. What is the color of the wind?
A. Blew.

A teacher asked, "Johnny, can you tell me the name of three great kings who have brought happiness and peace into people's lives?" Little Johnny responded, "Drin-king, smo-king, and f*c-king."

Q: What nails do carpenters hate to hit?
A: Fingernails.

Brunette: "Where were you born?"
Blonde: "California."
Brunette: "Which part?"
Blonde: "All of me."

Q: What do you call an alligator wearing a vest?
A: An investigator.

Q: What has more lives than a cat?
A: A frog because it croaks every night.

Q: What kind of car does Jesus drive?
A: A Christler.

Q: Why can't orphans play baseball?
A: Because they don't know where home is.

Q: What do you call a cow that just gave birth?
A: Decalfeinated.

A sailor drops anchor in a port and heads into the nearest pub. Everyone in the pub is whispering and pointing at him because of his odd shaped body; he has a very muscular body, but a very tiny head on his shoulders. As he orders his drink, he tells the bartender, "I'll explain. I get this in every port and town I visit. I caught a mermaid and she granted me three wishes if I would release her back into the sea. So I told her I wanted a yacht and, sure enough, she came through for me. Next, I asked for a million bucks and now I am set for life. Last of all, I asked her if I could have sex with her and her response was, 'I don't know how you can make love to me with your type of body.' So I asked her, 'How about a little head?'"

A man who is just married is flying to the Florida Keys for a business trip. His new bride is to accompany him the next day. When he gets there, he e-mails his wife to let her know he made it there safely. When he sends the e-mail, he mistypes the address. In Boston, a grieving widow, whose husband has recently passed away, receives the e-mail. She reads it, screams, and faints. Hearing her grandmother's cry, the widow's 18 year old granddaughter runs into the living room to see the computer on, with a message that reads, "Dear love, I just got here. Preparing for your arrival tomorrow. Can't wait to see you. Love, Me. P.S. Sure is hot down here."

Q: Why is the barn so noisy?
A: Because the cows have horns.

Q: What did the banana say to the doctor?
A: "I'm not peeling well."

Q: Why is Peter Pan always flying?
A: Because he neverlands.

For a period, Houdini used a trap door in every single show he did...I guess you could say it was a stage he was going through.

Q: If April showers bring may flowers, what do mayflowers bring?
A: Pilgrims!

Q: Why did the duck go to jail?
A: Because he got caught selling quack.

Q: What do you call a belt with a watch on it?
A: A waist of time.

A lot of people cry when they cut an onion. The trick is not to form an emotional bond.

Q: How do fish get high?
A: Seaweed.

A teacher asks her class what their favorite letter is. A student puts up his hand and says 'G'. The teacher walks over to him and says, "Why is that, Angus?"

Q: Why did the painting go to jail?
A: It was framed.

Three ladies were on a bus stop bench. One of the ladies looks at the other and asks her if she is Native American, She says, "Yes, I'm Arapaho." "Is that so?" says the first, "It just happens that I'm a Navajo." The third lady looks at both of them and says, "I'm a Dallas hoe."

Q: What do you call a Mexican that lost his car?
A: Carlos.

Q: What do cars eat on their toast?
A: Traffic jam.

Q: Why didn't the melons get married?

A: Because they cantaloupe.

Q: What did the hurricane say to the palm tree?
A: "Better hold onto your nuts because this is no ordinary blowjob."

Little Johnny came home from school and heard the word "b*tch." He asks his mom what the word meant and she responds, "It means priest." The next day little Johnny comes home and hears the word "sh*t" and asks his dad what it means. His dad answers, "It means food on the table." At school, he hears the word "f*cking" and asks his mom what it means. She responds, "It means getting ready." The next day a priest came over for dinner and little Johnny opened the door and says, "Hey son of a b*tch. There's sh*t on the table and my parents are upstairs f*cking!"

Two fish are in a tank. One turns to the other and says, "Hey, do you know how to drive this thing?"

Q: Why are hairdressers never late for work?
A: Because they know all the short cuts!

Bob goes to see his friend Pete. He finds Pete in his barn dancing naked around his John Deere. "What are you doing!" asks Bob. Pete stops dancing & says, "My wife has been ignoring me lately so I talked to my psychiatrist and he said I needed to do some thing sexy to a tractor." [to attract her]

Q: Why did the pig leave the costume party?
A: Because everyone thought he was a boar.

Q: Why can't your nose be 12 inches long?
A: Because then it'd be a foot!

Gandhi walked barefoot most of the time, which produced an

impressive set of calluses on his feet. He also ate very little, which made him rather frail and with his odd diet, he suffered from bad breath. This made him a super calloused fragile mystic hexed by halitosis.

A little kid was out trick-or-treating on Halloween dressed as a pirate. He rang a house's doorbell and the door was opened by a lady. "Oh, how cute! A little pirate! And where are your buccaneers?" she asked. The boy replied, "Under my buckin' hat."

Q: What did one hat say to another?
A: You stay here, I'll go on a head.

Q. Why did the apple run away?
A. Because the banana split!

Q: How do birds fly?
A: They just wing it!

There were two cannibals who captured a man. They decided it would be fair if they started eating from opposite ends. After a few minutes, the one who started at the head asked the other one, "How's it going down there?" And the other one replies, "I'm having a ball!"

Q: How can you get four suits for a dollar?
A: Buy a deck of cards.

Q: How do you make holy water?
A: Boil the hell out of it.

Teacher: "Where was the Constitution of India signed?"
Student: "At the bottom of the page!"

Q: What do you do with a sick boat?
A: Take it to the doc.

Why did Humpty Dumpty push his girlfriend off the wall?
So he could see her crack!

Q: Wanna hear a joke about construction?
A: Never mind, I'm still working on it.

The past, present, and future walked into a bar. It was tense.

Q: What did one ocean say to another ocean?
A: Nothing. It just waved.

Q: How do you make a witch itch?
A: Take away her "w".

A man speaks frantically into the phone, "My wife is
pregnant, and her contractions are only two minutes apart!"
"Is this her first child?" the doctor queries. "No, you idiot!" the
man shouts. "This is her husband!"

Q. What's a shark's favorite sandwich?
A. Peanut butter and jellyfish!

Q: Why did the runner stop listing to music?
A: Because she broke too many records.

Q: What do you call a woman that sets her bills on fire?
A: Bernadette.

Q: What's the importance of capitalization?
A: You can either help your Uncle Jack off a horse or help
your uncle jack off a horse.

Q. What did the pop star do when he locked himself out?
A. He sang until he found the right key!

Have you ever tried eating a clock? It's very time consuming.

Q: What did the spider do on the computer?

A: Made a website!

Q: What has four wheels and flies?
A: A garbage truck.

If money doesn't grow on trees, why do banks have branches?

Q: Why can't you tell an egg a joke?
A: Because it will crack up.

Q: Did you hear about the guy who drank 8 Cokes?
A: He burped 7Up.

Q: What did the judge say when a skunk walked into the courtroom?
A: "Odor in the court!"

Q: What city are you in when you drop your waffle on the beach?
A: Sandy Eggo.

How do you embarrass an archaeologist? Show him a used tampon and ask, "What period is this from?"

Two old friends crossed paths after not seeing one another for almost a decade.
Utkarsh: "What are you doing these days?"
Sparsh: "PHD."
Utkarsh: "Wow! You're a doctor!"
Sparsh: "No, Pizza Home Delivery."

Q: Why can't a bicycle stand up on its own?
A: Because it's two tired.

Q: Why do blonde girls walk in groups of odd numbers?
A: Because they can't even!

Q: What did the janitor yell when he jumped out of the closet?
A: "Supplies!"

Q: Why couldn't the Pirate learn the alphabet?
A: Because he was always lost at C.

Q: What do you call a famous fish?
A: A star fish.

Q: Why didn't the sailors play cards?
A: Because the captain was on the deck.

This crazy guy walks into a restaurant and tells the waiter, "Lemme get a cheeseburger, not too rare, not too well done, but right in the groove. Lemme get some fries, not too crispy, not too burnt, but right in the groove. And while you're at it, throw in a shake, not too thin, not too thick, but right in groove." The waiter took down the order and came back five minutes later and told the man, "The cook said you can kiss his ass, not to the left, not to the right, but right in the groove."

Q: Why do pirates not know the alphabet?
A: They always get stuck at "c."

Q: What did the pony say when he had a sore throat?
A: Sorry, I'm a little horse.

Q: Can a match box?
A: No, but a tin can.

Class trip to the Coca-Cola factory today. I hope there's no pop quiz.

Waiter: "Do you want any dessert?"
Teddy Bear: "No Thanks. I'm Stuffed!"

A man walks into a bar and sits down. He asks the bartender, "Can I have a cigarette?" The bartender replies, "Sure, the cigarette machine is over there." So he walks over to the machine and as he is about to order a cigarette, the machine suddenly says, "Oi, you bloody idiot." The man says with surprise in his voice, "That's not very nice." He returns to his bar stool without a cigarette and asks the bartender for some peanuts. The bartender passes the man a bowl of peanuts and the man hears one of the peanuts speak, "Ooh, I like your hair." The man says to the bartender, "Hey, what's going on here? Your cigarette machine is insulting me and this peanut is coming on to me. Why's this?" The bartender replies, "Oh, that's because the machine is out of order and the peanuts are complementary."

Q: What's the difference between America and yogurt?
A: If you leave yogurt alone for 200 years, it develops a culture.

Q: What do u call a seagull flying over the bay?
A: A bagel.

Q: What do you call a T-Rex's bruise? A: A dino-sore.

Did you hear about the butcher who backed up into the meat grinder? He got a little behind in his work.

Q: My boyfriend is as beautiful as Frank Sinatra and as intelligent as Albert Einstein; what is his name?
A: Frankenstein.

Teacher: "What is the largest city?"
Student: "Electricity!"

Q: How do you fix a broken tuba?

A: With a tuba glue.

Q: What did one wall say to the other wall?
A: "Meet you at the corner!"

Q: Why did the man take toilet paper to the party?
A: Because he was a party pooper.

What do you see when the Pillsbury Doughboy bends over?
Doughnuts!

Q: Why did they have to bury George Washington standing up?
A: Because he could never lie.

Q: How do you get a blond on the roof?
A: You tell her the food is on the house.

Q: Why is a river rich?
A: It has banks on both sides.

Why did the tomato turn red? Because he saw the salad dressing!

Q: What do you call a midget psychic who just escaped from prison?
A: A small medium at large.

Q: What does a lawyer wear to work?
A: A law suit.

Q: What starts with F and ends with U-C-K?
A: Firetruck.

Hickory Dickory Dock. Two mice ran up the clock. The clock struck one and the other got away with minor injuries.

Q: Why did the coach go back to the bank?

A: To get his quarterback!

A man is telling his neighbor, "I just bought a new hearing aid. It cost me $4000, but it's state of the art. It's perfect." "Really?" answers the neighbor. "What kind is it?" "12:30."

Q: Why did the man name his dogs Rolex and Timex?
A: Because they were watch dogs.

What do get if you cross a Snowman with a Vampire?
Frostbite.

Q: What did the grape say when it was stepped on?
A: Nothing, it just let out a little wine.

Q: What do you call a fish with no eyes?
A: A fsh.

Ya need an ark? I Noah guy.

Q: What Do You Call A Cow With No Legs
A: Ground Beef

Q: What does Mortal Kombat and a church in Helsinki have in common?
A: Finnish Hymn!

Have you heard the story of the magic sandwich? Never mind, it's just a bunch of bologna.

Q: What do you call a dinosaur with an extensive vocabulary?
A: A thesaurus.

Q: How do you get a baby alien to sleep?
A: You rocket.

Q: When the smog lifts in Los Angeles, what happens?

A: UCLA.

I'm in trouble with my next door neighbors. I went over to their house recently to jump on there tramperleen. I had just got on when I heard a voice say, "Hey you, get off my daughter Erleen!"

Q: Why are fish easy to weigh?
A: Because they have their own scales.

"Doctor, my nose is 11 inches long!"
"Come back when it grows into a foot!"

At last, the long-awaited finale of the televised poem competition had arrived.

The pope, who was a keen lyricist and writer of poems, had to everyone's surprise entered the competition. He immediately announced that he would only be reciting poems about personal spiritual experiences. Despite this limitation, it turned out he was gifted with words and he had made it all the way to the final. His opponent was the favorite to win: a Harvard linguistics professor on the top of his career and with a mind as sharp as a knife's edge.

The Harvard professor was up first. He was informed of the rules: "Two minutes to come up with a poem, and it must involve Timbuktu." The clock started, and when the time was up the Harvard professor approached the microphone:
"On my way through desert sand
Met a lonely caravan
Men on camels, two by two
Destination: Timbuktu."

The crowd went wild. Commentators were lyrical. This was

without a doubt the best poem of the competition. The Harvard professor had done it again! But as the crowd settled down their spirits sank. As far as anyone knew, the pope had never been to Timbuktu, which was soon confirmed by the TV commentator. How could the pope have a personal spiritual experience with such a word?!

The elderly pope was walked to the stage and informed of the same rules: "Two minutes to come up with a poem, and it must involve Timbuktu." The clock was started, but after only a short thought the pope stopped it. Everybody in the competition had used all the provided time, and as the pope approached the microphone a sigh went through the audience. Was he withdrawing from the competition? Would it all end in anti-climax?

No, to everybody's surprise the pope started to recite his poem based on personal spiritual experience:
"Me and Tim to Brisbane went
Met some ladies, cheap to rent.
They were three and we were two,
So I bucked one, and 'Tim-bucked-two.'"

What is the longest word in the English language? SMILES - There is a mile between the first and last letters!

The Taco Bell Chihuahua, a Doberman, and a Bulldog are in a bar having a drink, when a great looking female Collie comes up to them and says, "Whoever can say liver and cheese in a sentence can have me." So the Doberman says, "I love liver and cheese." The Collie replies, "That's not good enough." The Bulldog says, "I hate liver and cheese." She says, "That's not creative enough." Finally, the Chihuahua says, "Liver alone, cheese mine."

Q: Why is the space between a woman's breasts and her hips called a waist?
A: Because you could easily fit another pair of breasts there.

Fe = Iron.
Male = Man.
Fe + Male = Iron Man.
I have been having sex with Iron Man.

Q: Why did the kid throw the butter out the window?
A: To see the butter fly!

Q: What is the dirtiest line said on television?
A: "Ward, I think you were a little hard on the Beaver last night."

A blonde walks into a bar and asks the bartender, "What do you have on tap?" He replies, "Anheuser-Busch" (And-how's-your bush). She says, "Just fine. How's your penis?"

Q: What's the most expensive Jewish wine?
A: "I wanna go to Florida!"

Q: What's the difference between roast beef and pea soup?
A: You can roast beef but you cant pee soup.

What do you call four Mexicans in quicksand? Quatro sink-o!

Q: Why did the house go to the doctor?
A: It was having window pains.

A string walks into a bar and orders a drink. The bartender turns to him and says, "Sorry, sir, we don't serve strings here." The next day, clinging to a thread, the string returns to that same bar and orders a drink again. The bartender, resolute, again turns and says, "I'm sorry, sir, but like I said, we don't serve strings here. I'm going to have to ask you not to return." Dejected, the string returns home. All night he tosses and turns, wriggles and writhes, and awakes the next morning not at all resembling himself. Catching a glimpse of himself in the mirror, he brightens and jets out his door to that bar. Swaggering in, he orders a drink one more time. The bartender stares at him, squinty eyed, and asks, "I'm sorry, are you a string? You look very familiar." The string locks eyes with the bartender, and states, "No, sir. I'm a frayed knot."

Three old women were sitting on a park bench. A flasher ran up and whipped open his coat. Two of the old ladies had a stroke and the third couldn't reach.

Q: Why couldn't Dracula's wife get to sleep?
A: Because of his coffin.

Q: What did Gandhi say to the British, after they asked him to move?
A: Nah, mastay.

A man is filling up his car tank with gasoline and accidentally gets some on his hand. He doesn't notice it, so when he gets into his car he lights a cigarette. His arm instantly catches on fire. The man sticks his arm out the window and begins to wave it around attempting to blow out the flames crawling up his sleeve. A policeman sees the man struggling with his arm on fire and arrests him on the spot for an unlicensed firearm.

Q: How much does it cost a pirate to get his ears pierced?
A: A buccaneer!

To the optimist, the glass is half full. To the pessimist, the glass is half empty. To the engineer, the glass is twice as big as it needs to be.

Q: Where can you buy most of your chess pieces?
A: the pawn shop

What do you call a deer with no eyes? I have no I-Deer.

Just had a dangerous mole removed from the end of my penis. Definitely won't be shagging one of those again.

Q: Why couldn't the pirate play cards?

A: He was sitting on the deck.

A neutron walks into a bar and says, "I'd like a beer. How much will that be?" The bartender responds, "For you? No charge!"

Q: What did the fish say when he ran into a wall?
A: "Dam."

What did Pink Panther say when he stepped on an ant? "Dead ant, dead ant, dead ant, dead ant, dead ant."

Yo mamma is so fat that when she sat on a laptop, the hardware turned into software!

A drunk staggers out of a bar and lets go of a loud belch just as a couple are walking in the door. The man yells at the drunk, "How dare you belch before this woman!" The drunk says, "I'm sorry! I didn't know she wanted to go first."

A magician was driving down the road... then he turned into a driveway.

Q: What do you get when you cross a chicken and a vacuum?
A: A cocksucker.

Q: Why did the one armed man cross the road?

A: To get to the second hand shop.

Q: Did you hear abut the hungry clock?
A: It went back four seconds.

Q: Why did the scarecrow get a promotion?

A: Cause he was outstanding in his field.

I hate school and got caught skipping the other day. My principal said, "Walk normal next time, you fruitcake."

Q: What do you call a cow with two legs?
A: Lean beef.

Q: What do you do with epileptic lettuce?
A: You make a seizure salad.

Did you hear about the Italian chef that died? Yeah, he pasta way.

Q: What did the beaver say to the tree?
A: "It's been nice gnawing you!"

Don't trust atoms. They make up everything.

I'm thinking of becoming a hitman... I heard they make a killing.

Q: What did the storm say to the almond tree?
A: "Hold on to your nuts, cause you're about to get a blowjob."

Q: Where did the general keep his armies?
A: Up his sleevies.

Why did the hipster burn his mouth? Because he ate his pizza before it was cool.

My wife and I are planning our 21st wedding anniversary celebration. Here lies the problem: she wants to go to Outback Steakhouse, I want sex, and my mother-in-law thinks we should renew our vows at church. Well, I'm all for compromise, so we should have sex outback of the church.

Q: Which state has the most questions?
A: Alaska.

Knock, knock.
Who's there?
Yodelay hee.
Yodelay hee who?
I like your yodeling!

Q: What do you call a wandering caveman?
A: A meanderthal.

A naked man broke into a church. The police chased him around and finally caught him by the organ.

An American, a Vietnamese, a Mexican, a Brazilian, a Canadian, a German, a Turk, and a Russian walk into a fancy restaurant. When they got to the front desk, they were kicked out because they did not have a Thai.

Knock, knock.
Who's there?
Daisy.
Daisy who?
Daisy me rollin', they hatin'.

A husband says to his wife, "My Olympic condoms have arrived. I think I'll wear gold tonight." The wife replies, "Why not wear silver and come second for a change?""

Q: Why do pirates like algebra?

A: "Annex" marks the spot.

Q: What's the difference between a lentil and a chickpea?
A: I wouldn't pay $200 to have a lentil on my face.

A woman answered the doorbell with a man standing on her porch. The man said, "I'm terribly sorry. I just ran over your cat and I would like to replace it for you." The woman replied, "Well that's alright with me, but how are you at catching mice?"

Q. Why do anime fans listen to the radio in the morning?
A. Because they enjoy car toons!

Knock, knock.
Who's there?
Boo.
Boo who?
Don't cry. It's only a joke.

Q: What do you call two nuts on the wall?
A: Walnuts.
Q: What do you call two nuts on the chest? A: Chestnuts.
Q: What do you call two nuts on your chin?
A: A Blowjob.

Q. What's an astronaut's favorite social media website?

A. MySpace

Q: Why does a milking stool only have 3 legs?
A: Because the cow has the utter.

I didn't like my beard at first. Then it grew on me.

Q: Where can you find the biggest amount of the largest sized women's lingerie in the world?

A: In Africa: there's thousands of Z bras.

A church's bell ringer passed away. The church posted the job opening in the local newspaper's classified ads and a man came in with no arms wanting the job. The clergy weren't sure he could do it, but he convinced them to let him try it. They climbed the bell tower and the guy ran toward the bell and hit it with his head, producing a beautiful melody. They gave him the job on the spot. The next day he went to ring the bell, tripped, bounced off the bell and fell to the sidewalk below. Two priests were walking past. One asked, "Do you know this guy?" The other responded, "No, but his face rings a bell."
The next day, the dead man's twin brother came in for the again vacant bell ringer position. He also had no arms. The clergy led him up to the bell tower, where he ran at the bell, tripped and fell to the sidewalk below. The same two priests walked up. The first asked, "Do you know him?" The second responded, "No, but he's a dead ringer for his brother."

Q: How do convicts get drugs while they're in prison?
A: Some asshole brings 'em in.

Q: Why did the girl wear glasses in math class?
A: It improves di-vision.

Q: Why did the ink pots cry?
A: Their mother was in the pen doing a long sentence.

Knock, knock.
Who's there?
Madame.
Madame who?
Madame foot is caught in the door!

Fuddy: "I can't believe they are still together after all the shit

they have been through!"
Duddy: "Who?"
Fuddy: "My butt cheeks."

Q: What do you call a man that has no shins? A: Tony.

Q: What is brown and sticky?
A: A stick

What's the difference between roast beef and pea soup?
Anyone can roast beef but nobody can pee soup!

Q: What did the zombie girl say to the zombie boy?
A: "Are you going to kiss me or rot?"

Q: What do you call a duck that steals?
A: A Robber Duck.

Q: On what kind of ships do students study? A:
Scholarships.

Q: Why are there no televisions in Afghanistan?
A: Because of the Telly-ban!

Q: What do you get when you cross a donkey and an
onion?
A: A piece of ass that'll bring a tear to your eye.

Q: What's the difference between a voyeur and a thief?
A: A thief snatches your watch.

The Lone Ranger woke to see his tent blown away by a
tornado. He declared, "Tonto, we're not in canvas anymore."

Q: What do you get if you divide the circumference of a
pumpkin by its diameter?
A: Pumpkin Pi.

I met a one-legged woman outside of a club the other day. She was a bouncer.

Q: What do you call a snail who likes to sail?
A: A snailor!

19 Irishmen go to a cinema. Ticket lady says, "Why are there so many of you here tonight?" Mick replies, "The fillm says 18 and over, miss."

Why did Tigger stick his head in the toilet? He was looking for Pooh!

What did Matthew McConaughey say to the owl poachers? Owl rights, owl rights, owl rights.

Q: What do you call a noodle that commits identity theft?
A: An impasta!

Why does Snoop Dogg carry an umbrella? For drizzle!

Q: What is crazy and walks along the sides of buildings?
A: A walnut.

As I was walking down the street, I noted a man with a large pole in his hand and stopped to ask, "Are you a pole-vaulter?" His response was, "No, I'm German, but how did you know my name was Walter?"

The lord said unto John, "Come forth and receive eternal life," but john came fifth and won a toaster.

A man dining at a restaurant flagged down his waiter and said, "Excuse me. I have a bee in my soup." The waiter replied, "Yes sir. Didn't you order the alphabet soup?"

Q: Did you hear about the Buddhist who refused Novocaine during a root canal?

A: His goal: transcend dental medication.

Q: Did you hear about the kidnapping at school?
A: Its OK. He woke up.

The other night I played strip poker with my old lady: she stripped and I poked her.

Q: How did the ghost go on vacation?
A: By scareplane!

Q: What does a pirate pay for his corn?
A: A buck an ear (buccaneer).

Q: Why do milking stools only have three legs?
A: Because the cow's got the udder!

Q: Why were the Indians here first?
A: They had reservations.

Knock, knock.
Who's there?
Chicken.
Chicken who?
Chicken your pockets. I think the keys are in there.

Q: What do you call a vicar with a boner?
A: An erector.

Q: What do you call a girl with one leg?
A: Eileen.

Have you heard about the crime in multi-story parking decks? It's just wrong on so many levels.

A lawyer and a regular average Joe are on a plane together. The pilot comes on the speaker and announces that the flight will take up to 16 hours. The lawyer turns to Joe and says, "Okay, I have a game we can play while we pass the time. You ask me any question, and if I can't answer it, I'll give you $50. Then, I get to ask you a question, any question, and if you can't answer it, you give me $5." The average Joe says, "Okay, what has four legs going up a hill, and three legs at the bottom?" The lawyer thinks for a moment, then hands Joe $50 and says, "Wow, that was tough. I don't know, what does have four legs going up a hill and three legs at the bottom?" Joe then hands the lawyer $5 and says to him, "There's your $5."

Knock, knock.
Who's there?
Lettuce.
Lettuce who?
Lettuce in. It's cold outside.

Two Eskimos sitting in a kayak were chilly, so they lit a fire in the craft. Unsurprisingly it sank, proving once again that you can't have your kayak and heat it too.

A termite walks into a bar and says, "Where is the bar tender?"

Q: What did the verb say when the words have, has, and had were removed from the English language?
A: "Nobody's perfect!"

Q: Why did the ants dance on the jam jar?
A: The lid said, "Twist to open."

Never hit a man with glasses. Hit him with a baseball bat.

Q: If you go into the toilet American and you come out of the toilet American, what are you while you're on the toilet?
A: European.

Where do you get virgin wool? From ugly sheep.

A teacher was testing her students' knowledge of words' antonyms. She asked, "What is the opposite go?" A student answered, "Stop." "Very good," the teacher replied. "What is the opposite of adamant?" Another student said, "Eveant."

Q: Why did was the Mexican fast food vendor arrested?
A: He was planning a tacover.

I bet the butcher $50 that he couldn't reach the meat off the top shelf. He said, "No, the steaks are too high."

Becoming a vegetarian is a huge missed steak.

Q: Does a dolphin ever do something by accident? A: No, they do everything on porpoise.

There was a snake crossing a highway and a truck ran over its ass. The snake went back to get its ass and a truck ran over its head. The moral of the story is, "Don't lose your head over a piece of ass."

Knock Knock.
Who's there?
Olive.
Olive who?
Olive you!

Q: Why is a swordfish's nose 11 inches long?
A: Because if it were 12 inches long, it would be a foot!

There are 2 cats. The one two three cat and the un deux trois cat. They had a race across the English Channel. Which cat won? The one two three cat because the un deux trois cat cinq.

Q: What is the king of all inches?
A: The ruler.

What lies at the bottom of the ocean and twitches? A nervous wreck.

Knock, knock.
Who's there?
Abby.
Abby who?
Abby birthday!

Someone asked me, "Now that you are retired, do you still have a job?" I replied, "Yes I am my wife's sexual adviser." Somewhat shocked, they said, "I beg your pardon, but what do you mean by that?" "Very simple," I answered, "My wife has told me that when she wants my fucking advice, she'll ask me for it."

An English teacher wrote these words on the whiteboard, "Woman without her man is nothing." The teacher then asked the students to punctuate the words correctly. The men wrote, "Woman, without her man, is nothing." The women wrote, "Woman! Without her, man is nothing."

A man walked into a bar and heard, "Great tie!" He looked around and seeing no one, he heard again, "Beautiful suit!" Wondering what was going on, he saw the bartender walk up and said, "I heard a voice talking about my suit and tie, and that they looked cool, but no one's around. Dude, what's up?" The bartender smiled, "Oh yeah, those are the peanuts. They're complimentary!"

I just bought a cured ham; I wonder what it had.

Q: Wanna hear a joke about a stone?

A: Never mind, I will just skip that one.

A pirate walks into a bar and it appears that he has a steering wheel to a ship in front of his trousers. In fact, it looks like his penis is stuck through the center of it. The bartender says, "Hey pirate! You've got your penis stuck in a steering wheel!" The pirate replied, "Arrrr, I know! It drives me nuts!"

Q: What's an Indian's favorite sport?
A: Bolleyball.

Why is gambling illegal in Africa? Because there are too many cheetahs!

What do you call a piece of cheese that isn't yours? A: Nacho cheese.

Q: Why should you never trust a toilet?
A: Because it's full of shit.

Have you ever tried to eat a clock? It is very time consuming.

Conjunctivitis.com: a site for sore eyes.

Q: Why did the music teacher get arrested?
A: He fingered A minor.

A man said to his friend, "Want to hear a joke about butter?" His friend said, "Sure." The man said, "Nah, I butter not tell you. You might spread it."

Q: What did Saddam Hussein and Little Miss Muffit have in common?
A: They both had curds (Kurds) in their way (whey).

My mom drinks Diet Coke despite knowing full well of the repercussions to her health. You might say she's a sodamasochist.

Q: Why couldn't the kid see the pirate movie?
A: Because it was rated Rrrrr.

Q: What do you call it when you feed a stick of dynamite to a steer?

A: Abominable! (say it out loud, slowly)

Q: What's a frog's favorite drink?
A: Croak-a cola.

A man committed suicide by chopping his head off and left a suicide note in his mouth reading, "I don't need no body."

Q: What do the starship Enterprise and toilet paper have in common?
A: They both probe Uranus and wipe out Klingons.

Charles Dickens walks into a bar and asks for a martini. The bartender asks, "Olive or twist?"

In what state can you find small Pepsis? Mini-soda (Minnesota).

Knock knock.
Who's there?
Marry.
Marry who?
Marry me, please!

Q: What is the difference between a teacher and a train? A: The teacher says, "Spit out your gum," but a train says, "Chew chew!"

Two men walked into a bar. You would think at least one of

them would have ducked!

Q: Who was the smallest man in the Bible?
A: King David because he was only 12 inches tall as he was a ruler.

What did one butt cheek tell the other butt cheek? Don't cross the line.

Q: What goes up a chimney down, but cannot go down a chimney up?
A: An umbrella.

A tomato dad, mother, and son are walking in a street. The tomato son falls behind. The big father tomato walks back to the baby tomato, stomps on him, and yells, "Ketchup!"

Q: What do eggs do for fun?
A: Karayolke (karaoke).

What do you give a deaf fisherman? A herring aid.

Knock, knock.
Who's there?
Shelby.
Shelby who?
Shelby comin' around the mountain when she comes!

Q: What did the blanket say to the bed?
A: "I got you covered."

It'd be frustrating if you seriously couldn't find your friend Marco at a crowded swimming pool.

Two friends Peter and Jack are leaving for the holiday on the same airplane. Peter was sad when he couldn't meet Jack before they get in to the plane. After some time he sees Jack coming up down the aisle and Peter shouted, "HI-JACK!"

Where do pencils come from? Pencilvania.

Server: "What kind of ice cream do you want?" Muslim: "Allah the flavors."

Why was strawberry sad? Because her mom was in a jam.

How many tickles does it take to make an octopus laugh? Ten tickles (tentacles).

Did you hear about the dyslexic traffic cop who spent the weekend handing out IUD's?

I went to a drag race last Saturday. I still can't believe the guy in high heels won.

Q: Have you heard the joke about the trash can?
A: It's rubbish!

Q: Why did the cow cross the street? A: To get to the udder side.

Two peanuts are walking down the street when one was assaulted (a-salted).

Q: Why are pirates called pirates? A: Because they arrrr!

Q: What do you call a cow that eats your grass?
A: A lawn moo-er.

Bernie and Jane are an elderly couple who have decided to get married late in life. While they have not yet been intimate, Bernie thinks it would be a good idea to know how Jane feels about this. He asks her about her desires regarding frequency of sexual intimacy. Jane replies that she likes sex infrequently. Bernie, being ever the optimist says,

"Is that one word or two?"

Q: Where do crazy people travel through the forest?
A: The psycho path.

What do you call a girl with one leg? Eileen.

Little Bobby's teacher asked everyone to draw something exciting. Isabel drew a puppy, Jeffrey drew a cake, and little Bobby drew a period. The teacher looked puzzled and asked Bobby, "How is this exciting?" Bobby said, "Well it may not be to you, but my sister is missing two, so there is a lot of excitement at my house."

I drove my expensive car into a tree and found out how a Mercedes bends.

Where do you find a Zebra? 25 letters after A-Brah.

There are a lot of fish in the sea. Too bad I'm human.

A friend of mine got sacked from the dodgem cars; he's suing for funfair dismissal!

What's the biggest pencil in the world? Pennsylvania.

What do you call a cake made out of hamburgers? A patty cake!

A tourist from Romania visits New York City. He wanders around sightseeing and gets lost. He asks one of the locals for directions to get back to his hotel. The local notices the tourist's foreign accent and asks, "Are you by any chance Russian?" The Romanian replies, "No, I'm not really in a hurry."

How do you catch a unique rabbit? Unique up on it. How do you catch a tame rabbit? Tame way, unique up on it.

A turtle that was crossing the street was mugged one day. The policemen came to help and asked him what happened. He replied, "I am not sure, it happened too fast."

How are sex and bungee jumping related? When the rubber breaks, you're screwed!

Q: Why was six afraid of seven? A: Because seven is a registered six offender.

A man walks into a restaurant and sits down to order. The waiter walks up and takes the order. Before he is done taking his order, the waiter asks the man, "Would you like a soup or salad?" The man replies, "What's a super salad?"

"May I borrow your pen?"
"No, these are my special pens, and this is my second to last one"
"What's so special about them?"
"They are my ultimate writing instrument. I usually use them to keep track of the score in ultimate frisbee. Plus, they have famous people on them."
"Who is that?"
"That's Sean Penn. He's my favorite actor."
"Where did you get them?"
"At the University of Pennsylvania."
"Oh, I see. So that is your penultimate Penn ultimate Penn pen."

Why did the boy go out with a prune?
Because he couldn't find a date.

What's Mario's favorite fabric? Denim, denim, denim.

A man bursts into a psychiatrist's office, naked, with a thin sheet wrapped around his waist. The psychiatrist diagnoses,

"Sir, I can clearly see your nuts."

What are the best kind of letters to read in hot weather? Fan mail.

What did the mamma tomato say to the baby tomato? "Catch up!!!"

Why are buildings called buildings if they're finished? Shouldn't they be called builts?

The shortest word play joke ever. Dwarf shortage.

Why is the mushroom always invited to parties? Because he's a fungi!

What's the difference between pork chops and pea soup? Anyone can chop pork, no one can pea soup.

A Spanish man who doesn't speak English says to a Mexican woman, "Lady, I want to make the love with you," and she says, "Mande?" and he says, "No Monday, today."

Q: Why didn't the paraplegic look in the mirror?
A: He couldn't stand to see himself like that.

I was sitting in the traffic the other day. I got run over.

Q :How did Harry Potter get down the hill?
A: Walking......Jk,Rowling

What did the hat say to the scarf? "You hang around and I'll jump on a head."

Why did the sailor grab a piece of soap when he was sinking? So he could wash himself ashore

A fancy Alaskan restaurant invited a world famous chef to be a guest cook. Although the chef was renowned for his spectacular recipes, one customer asked him to prepare a local favorite: whale meat. Try as he might, everything the chef sent out just was not edible. The customer finally stormed back to the kitchen to berate the chef. The embarrassed chef offered to cook a meal of his finest recipes for the customer at no charge. After over an hour of preparation, the chef delivered to the diner the most magnificent gastronomic feast he had ever tasted. As he was leaving the restaurant, the satiated customer was overheard saying, "Well, that will teach me to never judge a cook by his blubber."

Q: What do you call a Mexican who lost his car ?

A: Carlos

Q: Why is it useless telling a shop keeper to be quiet?
A: Because they don't shut up until the end of the day.

Q: Where in L.A. can a deer hunter find does in season year round?
A: Venison Beach

What do you call a cow with big t*ts? An utter drag.

Did you hear about the drunk frog? He barley hops.

There are two eggs walking to an intersection. When they meet at the middle, one egg says to the other egg. Eggcuse me!

Here is a hipster pick up line. Hey girl, is that an original Yo La Tengo 7" in your pants? Because your butt is extremely valuable.

What kind of man is a mushroom? He's a fun guy!

Q: Why did the tomato blush?
A: Because it saw the salad dressing.

I never realized as I was growing up that our family didn't have much money. I thought all the girls wore full length pants in second grade and returned from summer wearing the same pants, but now we were calling them capris!

Q. Why couldn't the teddy bear eat his dessert?
A. Cause he was stuffed.

My little sister started to choke and my mom told me to heater in the back.

If con is the opposite of pro, then is Congress the opposite of progress?

Politicians and diapers have one thing in common: they should both be changed regularly... and for the same reason.

A worldwide survey was conducted by the UN. The only question asked was: "Would you please give your honest opinion about solutions to the food shortage in the rest of the world?" The survey was a huge failure. In Africa they didn't know what "food" meant. In Eastern Europe they didn't know what "honest" meant. In Western Europe they didn't know what "shortage" meant. In China they didn't know what "opinion" meant. In the Middle East they didn't know what "solution" meant. In South America they didn't know what "please" meant. And in the USA they didn't know what "the rest of the world" meant.

Three contractors are bidding to fix a broken fence at the White House. One is from Chicago, another is from Tennessee, and the third is from Minnesota. All three go with a White House official to examine the fence. The Minnesota contractor takes out a tape measure and does some measuring, then works some figures with a pencil. "Well," he says, "I figure the job will run about $900. $400 for materials, $400 for my crew, and $100 profit for me." The Tennessee contractor also does some measuring and figuring, then says, "I can do this job for $700. $300 for materials, $300 for my crew, and $100 profit for me." The Chicago contractor doesn't measure or figure, but leans over to the White House official and whispers, "$2,700." The official, incredulous, says, "You didn't even measure like the other guys! How did you come up with such a high figure?" The Chicago contractor whispers back, "$1000 for me, $1000 for you, and we hire the guy from Tennessee to fix the fence." "Done!" replies the government official. And that, my friends, is how the new stimulus plan will work.

Q: Have you heard about McDonald's new Obama Value Meal?
A: Order anything you like and the guy behind you has to pay for it.

A little boy goes to his dad and asks, "What is politics?" The dad says, "Well son, let me try to explain it this way: I'm the breadwinner of the family, so let's call me capitalism. Your mother, she's the administrator of the money, so we'll call her the government. We're here to take care of your needs, so we'll call you the people. The nanny, we'll consider her the working class. And your baby brother, we'll call him the future. Now, think about that and see if that makes sense." The little boy goes off to bed thinking about what dad had said. Later that night, he hears his baby brother crying, so he gets up to check on him. He finds that the baby has soiled his diaper. The little boy goes to his parents' room and finds his mother sound asleep. Not wanting to wake her, he goes to the nanny's room. Finding the door locked, he peeks in the keyhole and sees his father in bed with the nanny. He gives up and goes back to bed. The next morning, the little boy says to his father, "Dad, I think I understand the concept of politics now." The father says, "Good son, tell me in your own words what you think politics is all about." The little boy replies, "Well, while capitalism is screwing the working class, the government is sound asleep, the people are being ignored and the future is in deep shit."

I was walking down the street and I punched of a white guy and then I was arrested for assault. The next day after I got out, I punched a black guy and I was arrested for impersonating a police officer.

Q: Why is England the wettest country?
A: Because so many kings and queens have been reigning there.

When asked if they would have sex with Bill Clinton, 86% of women in D.C. said, "Not again."

Q: How many politicians does it take to change a light bulb?
A: Two: one to change it and another one to change it back again.

Did you hear about Monica Lewinsky becoming a Republican? The Democrats left a bad taste in her mouth.

Mahatma Gandhi often walked barefoot which produced an impressive set of callouses on his feet. He also ate very little, making him rather frail and with his odd diet he often suffered from bad breath. This made him a super calloused fragile mystic hexed with halitosis.

After numerous rounds of, "We don't know if Osama is still alive," Osama himself decided to send Ted Kennedy a letter in his own handwriting to let him know he was still in the game. Kennedy opened the letter which appeared to contain a single line of coded message, 370HSSV-0773H. Kennedy was baffled, so he e-mailed it to John Kerry. Kerry and his aides had no clue either, so they sent it to the FBI. Noone could solve it at the FBI, so it went to the CIA, then to the NSA. With no clue as to its meaning, the FBI finally asked Marine Corps Intelligence for help. Within a few seconds the Marine Corps cabled back with this reply, "Tell Kennedy he's holding the message upside down."

George W. Bush and his VP running mate, Dick Cheney, were talking, when George W. said, "I hate all the dumb jokes people tell about me." Wise Old Cheney, feeling sorry for his old boss, said sage-like, "Oh, they are only jokes. There are a lot of stupid people out there. Here, I'll prove it to you." Cheney took George W. outside and hailed a taxi driver. "Please take me to 29 Nickel Street to see if I'm home," said Cheney. The cab driver, without saying a word, drove them to Nickel Street, and when they finally got out, Cheney looked at George W. and said, "See! That guy was really stupid!" "No kidding," replied George W., "There was a pay phone just around the corner. You could have called instead."

Q: What do you call a lawyer who has gone bad?
A: Politician.

Bill Clinton and the Pope both died on the same day. Due to a minor clerical error, the Pope went to Hell, while Clinton went to Heaven. When the Pope arrived in Hell, everyone realized the mistake. Due to an issue with the union, they couldn't swap the two until the next day, and the Pope had to spend the night in Hell, while Clinton spent the night in Heaven. The next day the paperwork got worked out. On his way up to Heaven, the Pope ran into Clinton. Clinton asked the Pope, "How was your night in Hell?" "Very educational," responded the Pope. "I've learned a lot from the experience, but now I'm glad I'm going to Heaven. I've been waiting all my life to meet the Virgin Mary." "Ooh, sorry," said Clinton, "you should have been there yesterday."

Monica Lewinsky walks into the dry cleaners. The old man behind the counter is hard of hearing and doesn't understand her request, so he says, "Come again." Monica responds, "No, this time it's mustard."

Q: What do you call a lawyer with an IQ of 100?
A: Your Honor.
Q: What do you call a lawyer with an IQ of 50?
A: Senator.

Q: Whats the difference between a politician and a snail?
A: One is slimy, a pest, and leaves a trail everywhere and the other is a snail.

A Scotsman who was driving home one night, ran into a car driven by an Englishman. The Scotsman got out of the car to apologize and offered the Englishman a drink from a bottle of whisky. The Englishman was glad to have a drink. "Go on," said the Scot, "have another drink." The Englishman drank gratefully. "But don't you want one, too?" he asked the Scotsman. "Perhaps," replied the Scotsman, "after the police have gone."

What happens when you give a politician Viagra? He gets taller.

It was so cold today, a Democrat had his hands in his own

pockets!

Made in the USA
Coppell, TX
13 July 2023

19057209R10111